MAURICE WILSON

A YORKSHIREMAN ON EVEREST

MAURICE WILSON

A YORKSHIREMAN ON EVEREST

Ruth Hanson

HAYLOFT

First published 2008

Hayloft Publishing Ltd, Kirkby Stephen, Cumbria, CA17 4DJ

tel: + 44 (0) 17683) 42300
fax. + 44 (0) 17683) 41568
e-mail: books@hayloft.eu
web: www.hayloft.eu

ISBN 1 904524 56 7

A catalogue record for this book is available
from the British Library

Printed and bound in the EU

Papers used by Hayloft are natural, recyclable products made from wood grown in
sustainable forests. The manufacturing processes conform to the environmental
regulations of the country of origin.

For George, with love.

FOREWORD

Maurice Wilson, 'a Yorkshireman on Everest' was very much the quintessential Yorkshireman, tough, sentimental, stubborn, honest and certain of himself – convinced – and this one prepared to die for his conviction and did.

Ruth Hanson has written wonderfully well of Maurice Wilson admitting to have been touched by his 'courage, some altruistic intention and a whole hearted strength of purpose.' I found the whole story quite compelling, a real page turner needing to know more of this eccentric Englishman's efforts to show the world how to live by climbing Everest alone.

By 1932 Maurice Wilson was in decline; most likely he was unable to strike a balance after suffering two horrendous teenage years fighting in the trenches of the First World War. He went through two failed marriages and eventually had all the symptoms of depression and TB. He came across a healer who advised him to fast for 35 days, to drink only a few sips of water and to pray to God to be reborn. He followed the instructions implicitly, became mentally strong enough to take himself off to the Black Forest to fully recuperate and to regain his prodigious physical strength. For the first time in years he knew peace and happiness. It is a characteristic of mankind to immediately try to turn the rest of us on to what has suddenly lifted the spirit.

Maurice Wilson was aware of all the suffering and misery in the world, and of the great difficulty facing him in spreading the word that he had found the answer. How would he convince the rest of Mankind of the efficiency of his new found faith? He was soon to be in his thirty fifth year – a time when all men are at the height of their physical strength and endurance and traditionally a time for spiritual revelation.

It was in a café in Freiburg that he suddenly realised what he had to do, how he could harness his physical strength and spiritual awareness for the benefit of the whole world – he would climb Everest solo. He had no interest in mountains themselves but an article on the disappearance of Mallory and Irvine in 1924 did catch his attention and fired his imagination to do what a large official expedition had dramatically failed to do. If he could succeed alone that would make the rest of the world sit up and take note of the power of his faith. So in the beginning at least his motivation was to spontaneously share and care for others – that's not a bad thing.

How this wonderful mad idea was attempted is only made more fantastic when Maurice Wilson, not only a non-climber but also not a pilot, decides to fly out to Everest solo in a Gypsy Moth bi-plane named *Ever Wrest* to be crash landed on the Rongbuk Glacier!

The author is not herself a pilot nor a mountaineer, but has nevertheless written refreshing accounts of both flying and mountaineering in the 1930s. She also writes interesting background to the Asian politics of the time and Tibetan Buddhism especially in the Rongbuk Valley which she herself visited.

With all the odds stacked up against him Wilson flew *Ever Wrest* out to India. He had defeated the long reach of hostile British Authority, coped with hours of brain numbing boredom, flying through storms, and coping with fuel shortage, bumpy landings but never flinching from his goal, writing later of Middle East officialdom: 'Well Everest wasn't Cairo so on I pushed to Baghdad.'

Having arrived in India he makes a promise which is kept not to fly over Nepal and on to the Rongbuk Glacier – Tibet. He therefore makes his way to Darjeeling from where, in disguise, he will walk to Everest Base Camp. This he does despite more problems with the authorities and the rigours of the Tibetan Plateau. Maurice Wilson in fact chops ten days off the previous journey time. This is a journey on which expedition climbers have perished. No wonder Maurice Wilson thought he was in with a chance to 'set the World alight' having made such good time with no back up, having to keep his head down avoiding local town and village authorities with only three Sherpa companions he had taken on in Darjeeling.

At Rongbuk he had 'a damned good bath and rub down' and congratulated himself in his diary for having got so far without ever putting on woollen clothing, 'am now feeling the benefit.' There is no telling what Maurice Wilson might have achieved as a climber on a regular mountaineering expedition. He was obviously very strong and well able to acclimatise to cold and altitude.

Unfortunately he was not a mountaineer, had only made endurance walks from London to Bradford in preparation, and was completely out of his depth when it came to glacier travel and climbing up to the North Col.

It was on the slopes below the col that Shipton's 1935 party discovered his corpse and diary.

He had pushed himself past the point when he could still rationalise his true position. Altitude can do that to people especially those not familiar with the effect of lack of oxygen on the brain and being of man.

He did not have a 'death wish' as evidenced by his diary entries. One about his Mother reads, 'Am going to take her round all the old childhood spots when I get back.' Nor did he shun his fellow men – he knew the joy of human friendship and missed it on the mountain. He records returning from his self-imposed isolation after his first attempt to reach the North Col, 'Tewang rushed with outstretched hands and a row of snow white teeth in a smiling face. Next came Tsering in thick night attire, also with a glad smile, followed by Rinzing. 'All delighted'.'

Just as the Sherpas helped Maurice Wilson so much, they

have also given me sterling service throughout all my climbing career (35 years of Himalayan climbing). Hence the inspiration fifteen years ago to start Community Action Nepal to help these guys and their families.

Doug Scott, CBE.
Spring, 2008.

ACKNOWLEDGEMENTS

Many people and organisations have helped in different ways to move this book from my vague idea to the reality of print; and I thank them all. However I am grateful to the following in particular:

Dawn Robertson at Hayloft, for editing and assembling the text and pictures, but most of all for her support, patience and enthusiastic belief in the project throughout.

Audrey Salkeld for generously letting me review the documents she has about Maurice Wilson in her Everest files; and especially for her interest and encouraging suggestions.

Glyn Hughes, and his colleagues at the Alpine Club Library, for allowing me access to the information and records they hold about both Maurice Wilson and the 1935 Everest expedition.

Doug Scott for agreeing to contribute the foreword.

Ralph Steiner, at the de Havilland Aircraft Heritage Centre, for providing a photograph of a Gypsy Moth similar to *Ever Wrest* for use in the book.

Justin Hobson and Joy Wheeler, of the Royal Geographical Society, for letting me see some of the original pictures from the early Everest expeditions in the Society's archives, and agreeing to the use of those reproduced in my book.

Jenny White-Cooper for the wonderful maps.

Dominic Webster of the *Daily Mail* for responding positively to my tentative enquiry to several newspapers, and sending me a treasure-trove packet of copy articles.

Friends I have travelled with, and the many different people I have met on my various treks and trips to countries in the Himalayas. Without them I could have not have seen, appreciated, learned or experienced so much, and my life would have been poorer as a result.

Last but not least, my Mum for believing I could finish this book; and George, Elaine and Crispin for supporting and encouraging me all the way, and for their feedback on my first draft.

CONTENTS

Maurice Wilson, the soldier.

THEY CALLED HIM
'THE MAD YORKSHIREMAN'

If you can force your heart and nerve and sinew
To serve your turn long after they are gone,
And so hold on when there is nothing in you
Except the Will which says to them: 'Hold on!'
                              Rudyard Kipling

Climbing Mount Everest alone. It sounds like a scheme dreamed up in a bar at the end of a long night; but Maurice Wilson was teetotal, kept out of pubs and really meant it – to fly to Tibet, land on the mountain's lower slopes, continue on foot and become the first man to reach the top. He had no climbing experience and could not fly, but he believed it was his destiny, and that God would guide his feet up the Himalayan rocks and glaciers.

I first heard about Maurice Wilson while on holiday in Scotland with friends one New Year. Curled up with tea and toasted crumpets after an icy walk, I was browsing through a book about Everest that one of us had been given for Christmas when a faded photograph caught my eye. It showed a man standing in front of a small bi-plane; hands on hips, wearing a leather helmet and flying goggles, and staring at the camera with a quizzical half smile. I read the piece, and something about Maurice Wilson caught my imagination. Perhaps it was the crazy impossibility of his plan; or knowing he got as far as he did when most people – including myself – would have given it up as hopeless; or even our shared Yorkshire roots.

The more I found out about him, the more he got under my skin. I came to admire things about him. Yes he was audacious, egotistical and eccentric, and I can well understand why the 1930s press dubbed him 'The Mad Yorkshireman'. Either naively or recklessly he underestimated the difficulty of the climb, and relied too absolutely on his faith, so making no effort to learn skills that could have helped him. I imagine he was frustratingly stubborn, uncompromising and unbending. But he also had courage, some altruistic intention and a wholehearted strength of purpose. I am conscious that he had no more climbing experience than me, and so, although he is one of the many who have tried and failed to reach the highest point on earth, I find his story at the same time fascinating and touching; and his achievement stands testament to both his faith and his self belief. I feel there is something about people who strive to make their dreams a reality that speaks to all of us, whatever our circumstances. For me, Maurice Wilson is one of them. He was on Everest in 1934, ten years after Mallory and Irvine's famous climb, and sandwiched between a succession of official expeditions drawn from some of the most experienced climbers of the time, but it took another nineteen years before Hillary and Tenzing both reached the summit and came back to tell the tale.

Maurice Wilson was born in Bradford on 21 April 1898, one of four brothers. His parents, Mark and Sarah Wilson, were known in the area for their charitable work amongst the poor, who struggled to make ends meet in the cramped and smoky streets that stretched up the hill to Great Horton. Mark Wilson, who had been a worsted weaver's overlooker when Maurice was born, worked his way up to be a wool manufacturer, principal of Mark Wilson Limited of Holme Top Mills.

Not unusually he hoped his sons would join him in textiles and Maurice Wilson started his apprenticeship in 1914.

As it did with so many families' comfortable plans, the First World War blew Mark Wilson's ambitions for his son away. In April 1916, having reached eighteen, Maurice Wilson enlisted as a private in the 5th Battalion of the West Yorkshire Regiment (the Prince of Wales' Own). After training in physical discipline, field skills, weapon handling and leadership, followed by months of exercises in England and then promotion, he was commissioned as a second lieutenant, and sent to France in 1917.

His regiment formed part of the 146th Infantry Brigade (49th Division) fighting that year's long battles at Ypres. Maurice Wilson became one of the brotherhood known within the Forces as the PBI, 'Poor Bloody Infantry'; not only did they have the deadliest role in the front line, but they also shouldered the burden of much gruelling physical work, fetching and carrying, as well as clearing trenches, repairing their wooden and sandbag walls and laying barbed wire. The general pattern of routine was four days in the front line, four days in reserve in trenches behind the thick of the action, and then four days at rest. However, this often varied with the intensity of the fighting, weather and ground conditions, as well as the availability of enough troops for some to be held in reserve. Men were crowded together in a bog of bodies, sickness and vermin, sitting out long hours of boredom broken by orders to action and everything combat meant.

Maurice Wilson was awarded the Military Cross for his part in this desperate fighting. All the First World War award of gallantry medals were notified in the Official Gazettes, which are available on the internet now. Grappling with the search facility, I finally and triumphantly found Maurice Wilson's medal listed the following year in one of the supplements to the *London Gazette* of 13 September 1918. There is one paragraph on hundreds of sheets of so many men's

names, each with a brief, close-typed account below. Even
on a computer screen I found that those old pages, with their
snapshot entries, give as poignant an image of that dark time,
as the pictures we see of neat lines of war graves. Each just
states the bald, bare facts of one man's story. Maurice
Wilson's particular note reads:

> *2nd Lt Maurice Wilson, W York R*
> *For conspicuous gallantry and devotion to duty. He*
> *held a post in advance of the line under very heavy*
> *shell and machine-gun fire on both flanks after the*
> *machine guns covering his flanks had been withdrawn.*
> *It was largely owing to his pluck and determination in*
> *holding this post that the enemy attack was held up.*[1]

After this incident, but still during his time at Ypres,
Maurice Wilson was seriously injured by machine gun fire
and spent some months recovering in hospital, first in France
and then back in England. Although he was well enough to
rejoin his regiment and serve as a captain until the armistice,
his weak left arm never fully healed, and it was to give him a
lot of pain for the rest of his life.

Imagining the mud, horror and death of the trenches I find
it easy to understand why Maurice Wilson struggled to adapt
to a humdrum routine in the Bradford textile trade. He knew
now that the world had wider horizons, and found that his
thoughts, feelings and memories had followed him home
from France. Perhaps trying to build an ordinary normality,
to find some security, or maybe even to ease his mother's
worries for him after the death of his father, he married
Beatrice Hardy Slater. The ceremony took place at St John's
Church, Great Horton on 20th July 1922. He was 24,
described as a merchant on the entry in the marriage register,
and his bride was 22. But wedding bells are no guarantee of

happiness, and whatever love the couple shared, it did not tie Maurice Wilson to Yorkshire.

He moved to London, where he stayed for a while, before emigrating – drifting first to America and then on to New Zealand where, after a spell at farming, he ran a successful dress shop in Wellington. There his marriage to Beatrice ended in divorce in February 1926, and four days later he married Ruby Russell, who was originally from Tasmania, but also lived in Wellington.

But again it was not enough, and a few years later Maurice Wilson suddenly decided to leave his new country, catching a mail boat back to England. No doubt hoping his wandering was at an end, his mother and brothers welcomed him home, but Maurice Wilson chose to live and work in London. He hoped to make a fresh start but, unsettled and low, wondered what he had achieved so far, what he was looking for in life and what it all meant.

Although he was familiar with London, and knew some people there, his strongest friendship grew with new acquaintances Leonard and Enid Evans. He had met Leonard Evans when buying a car, but their relationship quickly moved from business to a social one. The three of them formed a strong and affectionate bond, and spent a great deal of time together.

Some months after he had moved back to London, Maurice Wilson became quite ill. Grappling with a racking cough that most likely signalled TB, and quite possibly suffering from depression too, he lost weight, his bleak, unhappy eyes sank into hollow cheeks and each day felt more of a grim, grey struggle than the one before.

In desperation he consulted a healer, who advised him to fast for 35 days, drinking only a little water, and to pray to God to be reborn. Retreating from his usual day-to-day activities, Maurice Wilson followed these instructions to the letter, keeping in silence and prayer, and searching within himself for faith and an answer. Finally he felt ready to face the world again – physically weak but, without his dark and over-whelming sadness, mentally stronger than he had been for years. Almost not daring to hope that he was climbing back out of his private pit, he allowed himself a couple of months off and travelled to the Black Forest to recuperate.

While he was there he found that each day he felt fitter, happier and more at peace; his cure had been successful; he was enjoying himself; life was good after all. Slowly he became convinced that if faith had helped him so much, it could help others too. Perhaps he also remembered the quiet strength and simplicity of the Indian yogis he had met on his sea journey back from New Zealand. Throughout the world there was misery and suffering, and now Maurice Wilson felt sure that if people only had enough faith things could change. The difficulty was how to convince millions of sceptical individuals that this was the answer.

It was during his convalescence trip to Germany that the focus of Maurice Wilson's life shifted dramatically. While in a café in Freiburg he happened across a tattered, jam stained article about the 1924 Everest expedition and the disappearance of Mallory and Irvine. Although he did not feel the pull of the high hills himself, the piece gave him a sudden flash of inspiration. If faith could move mountains, then it could help men climb mountains – more particularly, it could help one man climb one mountain. And if one man could succeed where a whole expedition had so publicly failed, then what more proof of the absolute power of faith would the world need?

In the end Maurice Wilson was to give his life trying to show the world how to live. But like many single-minded people his determination and focus were so complete that he could not accept when enough was enough; he could not bear to be beaten, either by the forces of nature, or by admitting his own lack of climbing skill, and so he let what he had first intended to be his way of demonstrating faith – a means to an end - become his all consuming goal. But if he had been otherwise I suspect he would never have reached Tibet. Whether he was mad, brave, naively stupid, or all three, his first motivation was a generous one. Of course his complex character was driven by others too – fame, ambition and ego; to be the first and to 'set the world on fire'. I think it says a lot about the man that his ultimate ambition, his post Everest project, was to build a flying machine that would take him beyond the earth's atmosphere.

When Maurice Wilson left London for Tibet he entrusted all his papers to Leonard and Enid Evans, who he also made his executors. The diary, which was found with his body, is a small, plain, hardcover notebook that he bought in Darjeeling, and roughly half of its pages are covered with his sloping pencil handwriting. He jotted the words 'Flying Thoughts' next to the opening page. There are also some illegible words after the figure '3', and I wonder if he had already filled two notebooks since the start of his trip – maybe one about his flight and the other telling of his experiences in India – and sent them back to Leonard and Enid Evans in London, probably with his flying log too? Parts of his diary read as though he was writing to his friends, and especially to Enid, who was particularly dear to him.

This notebook was acquired by Mr L E Frank, and given to the Alpine Club in 1965. It is kept in the Club's archives in London, and is a fascinating but frustrating document. There are detailed accounts of some things. For example, Maurice Wilson recorded almost obsessively what he ate (although those who have trekked or climbed in the Himalayas may empathise with this). But there are very few descriptions of the countryside he passed through or what he saw, and even less about how he felt. Everything, even his pencil, was focussed on getting to the summit. Fortunately for those of us trying to get a broader and more colourful picture of what his march to Tibet and attempts on the mountain might have been like, some members of the early Everest expeditions wrote vividly and extensively about their experiences, and their books are invaluable.

I found picking through Maurice Wilson's text both gripping and moving. At first I was surprised to find he had written it in pencil – but then discovered that biro pens were not produced commercially until 1945, and ink for a fountain pen would have been a messy liability at lower altitudes, and liable to freeze up on the mountain. Some of the diary is illegible, although that is not surprising after all this time, particularly as it was exposed to the elements for a year before members of the 1935 expedition happened upon his body. Squinting through a magnifying glass I could just about make out most of his cramped, spiky handwriting – and it feels as though Maurice Wilson is speaking through the years, telling his story, sometimes sharing his thoughts but sometimes not. At times I felt I was eavesdropping, for his words had not been written for me to read; and, knowing what the future had in store, I found it chilling to look at his entries over the last few days. A voice inside me wanted to tell him to stop and turn back – but it was too late; all I could do was read on and watch his story run its course.

But I am jumping ahead. At this point, 1932, it is the beginning of Maurice Wilson's Everest story that matters.

MOUNTAIN, MYTHS AND MYSTERY

*To the wilderness, to Chomolungma's glacier
walls, I went, craving solitude.*

Milarepa

There is something about Everest, Chomolungma to the
Tibetans, Goddess Mother – the highest point in the world. It
represents something, even to those who do not love the
mountains. And to those of us who do, for many different
reasons, it has a pull and a fascination, even when there are
other peaks closer to our hearts.

These days it feels quite familiar, from newspapers, books,
films and, for a fortunate few, our own experience, and I find
it hard not to take this for granted. But for thousands of years
it was unacknowledged – just one in a close crowd of high
mountains.

The Himalayas are vast, about half as long as the Atlantic
is wide, with more than a hundred peaks over 24,000ft
(7,315m) above sea level and twenty over 26,000ft (7,925m).
The range cuts across Asia, dividing countries, peoples, cli-
mates and ways of life. To the south of the mountains the
land is lush, there are forests, fields and farms supported by
the monsoon rains and steady heat. To the north the climate
is dry and arid, with extremes of temperature from baking hot
to desperate cold, there are hardly any trees, only sparse vegetation and few fields, with nomadic people moving their animals around the more temperate areas in search of grazing
land. It is a natural barrier, discouraging invaders from either

side, and it is the source of the great rivers that support the civilisations of much of Asia – the Yangtze, Irrawaddy, Ganges, Indus and Brahmaputra. For this gift of life, even those who are too far away to see the mountains hold the high Himalaya in reverence, for it is the source of mother Ganga and the place of ancient, sacred peaks, such as Meru, Machhupuchare and Kailas, home of Lord Shiva. Traditionally, only pilgrims, ascetics and holy men sought to travel there.

In the nineteenth century, as some of the European nations reached eastwards looking for land and trade, two countries protected themselves, adding to the natural defence of the mountains and their inhospitable climate by closing their borders. The kingdom of Nepal refused access to Westerners from 1815 to 1945, and Tibet, under the rule of the Dalai Lamas, held out for almost as long. However it was during this time that the extent of the Himalayan range, and the height of its great peaks, was first realised. In 1784, Sir William Jones proposed that they were further from India than it appeared, and must therefore be taller than the Andes (which were then accepted as the highest mountains in the world). At the time this, and similar claims, were pooh poohed by the scientific establishment.

Along with the drive for power and profit, the nineteenth century Europeans cultivated science and discovery. All over the world different people were observing, recording, measuring, documenting and collecting – plants, animals, rocks and birds. Between 1817 and 1820, John Hodgson and William Webb carried out some surveys from northern India, trekking into the mountains to the west of Nepal, identifying and measuring Nanda Devi (25,645ft; 7,817m), and claiming it to be higher than anywhere in the Andes.

It remained the highest identified peak for over thirty

years, as, bit by bit, the great trigonometrical survey of India was completed. This was an immense undertaking, spanning the continent as British influence strengthened and extended. It began under the leadership of William Lambton, who was interested in studying the physical shape of the landscape and wanted to work out the curvature of the earth. He carried out measurements in an arc from Madras, in southern India, up 1,600 miles (over 2,550km) to the Himalayas, although this was later extended to include all of Kashmir. His theodolite weighed over half a ton and needed twelve men to carry it. Following Lambton's death in 1823 George Everest took up the stewardship of the survey. Measurements of the southern half of the arc that Lambton had planned were essentially complete, but the challenge of the mountains was still to come.

George Everest was Surveyor General of India until 1843, when he handed the task to Andrew Waugh. As the survey moved towards India's northern frontier, local men, known as pundits (from the Hindi word 'pandit', meaning teacher), were employed to travel to remote and sometimes forbidden areas, collecting measurements and information. The pundits were often disguised as pilgrims or holy men to avoid suspicion, using prayer beads to help them count distances and hiding their records inside handheld prayer wheels.

Andrew Waugh calculated that Kangchenjunga was higher than Nanda Devi, but he kept this to himself as further sightings, in 1847 and 1849, suggested that another peak, beyond Kangchenjunga, was higher still. He got his staff to check and recheck the measurements, relying on the Bengali mathematical genius, Radhanath Sickdhar, to put it beyond all doubt – in 1856, peak XV in the survey's records, at 29,002ft (8,840m) was declared the highest mountain in the world.

The only question then was its name. The survey's tradition was to use local names, when they were known, but Waugh insisted that it should be called after his predecessor.

The debate raged. There were several possible local names, Chomolungma and Tschoumou-Lanckma were used in Tibet, while Devadhunka and Chingopanmari were known in Nepal. However, Waugh held out, and peak XV was officially called Mount Everest.

These days the mountain is known by several names – Everest and Chomolungma, but also Sagarmatha, a Sanskrit word meaning Head of the Sky, given to it by the Nepali government after it was established as the highest mountain on earth. More recently the Chinese have put their own spin on place-names in Tibet and use Qomolangma.

There has also been debate over the precise meaning of Chomolungma – the most common one is Goddess Mother of the World, but others are Land of the Hen Birds, Lady Cow, the Peak above the Valley and Lady Langma; Langma being short for Miyolangsangma, the goddess who is believed to live on the mountain.

❀ ❀ ❀ ❀ ❀ ❀ ❀

For the second half of the nineteenth century, it was enough that the highest mountain had been identified, measured and named. By 1860 one of the British Empire's major concerns was protecting India from threats beyond its inhospitable northern frontier, mindful of the power of both Czarist Russia and Imperial China. This was the so-called Great Game. Trying to find out more about the mountains, their snowy passes and what lay beyond them, the pundits risked journeys further across Tibet and into central Asia. It was time consuming, painstaking and dangerous work, but over many years these men brought and sent back invaluable information for the mapmakers and politicians. The army's covert missions included the ambitious and intrepid Francis Younghusband roaming north of the Karakoram, spying in the name of science. The story goes that Younghusband and one of his army colleagues, Charles Bruce, discussed whether an ascent of Everest might be possible, although at the time mountaineering as a sport was in its infancy and there were still many unclimbed peaks in Europe. Whether or not the fabled conversation actually happened, both men were to later play their own part in Everest's history.

In 1903, with the Empire's authorities still fearful of Russian influence, a British delegation was sent to Tibet to negotiate both politics and trade with His Holiness the Thirteenth Dalai Lama and his ruling lamas and dzongpens. Francis Younghusband, who by then had reached the rank of Colonel, was given charge of the mission's military escort. At the border the Tibetans refused them admission. The delegation marched on regardless and its escort became an army, subduing the ill equipped and inexperienced Tibetans in a bloody show of force for which Younghusband has been much criticised. But in setting out the terms of the later truce he required a clause giving Britain access to the central Himalayan peaks through Tibet. And so, with Nepal still firmly closed to foreigners, the route and nationality of the first expeditions to Everest was determined.

Following the First World War the Royal Geographical Society and the Alpine Club joined forces in London to establish the Mount Everest Committee, under Younghusband's direction. In 1920, negotiations for an exploratory expedition to the Everest region were opened with the Dalai Lama. The Committee's hope was that a team would establish a route to Everest, study the geology and wildlife, draw up detailed maps and look for a way up the mountain. At the time it was not known whether people could even live at such a great altitude. An Italian expedition had made it up to 24,000ft (7,315m) in the Karakoram, but considered that survival beyond that height was unlikely. In addition, no one knew what technical difficulties might be involved, either in getting to Everest or in trying to climb it. When the 1921 expedition left England, led by Charles Howard-Bury, its members and sponsors truly had no idea of what might be in store.

They also did not fully appreciate how their Western approach of exploring, cataloguing and conquering the physical world was diametrically opposite to the cultural roots of the people of the Himalaya. In 1921, most ordinary Tibetans had a physically tough life of farming and herding and, devoutly Buddhist, any spare resources or energy were invested in their faith – supporting monasteries, going on pilgrimages, following the path to enlightenment.

Seen from that point of view, climbing a mountain 'Because it's there' (as George Mallory once famously said) is unnecessary. The Tibetans saw the mountains as sacred places, with gods and goddesses inhabiting some of the highest peaks. Climbing their slopes could disturb the deities. Pilgrims still circumnavigate the base of perhaps the most holy peak, Mt Kailas, prostrating full length as they go, to gain merit; and if it is necessary to climb over a pass during a journey Tibetans traditionally burn juniper, build stone cairns as a peace offering, and hang prayer flags to fill the wind with wishes for the enlightenment of all.

In old Tibet, only those going in peace, seeking closeness to holy places, spent time deep in the mountains. Monks, nuns and yogis lived for years in tiny caves, in self imposed exile, silence, cold and near starvation, meditating, praying and searching for inner knowledge. Many years later, in an introductory message for a book commemorating the 50th anniversary of the successful ascent of Everest, His Holiness the Fourteenth Dalai Lama gave the gentle reminder that, 'in Tibet we remember Milarepa for meditating on her slopes and conquering the mind.'[1]

Although saddened by the death of their doctor and experienced Himalayan mountaineer, Alexander Kellas, shortly after they entered Tibet, the 1921 expedition was successful in reaching the foot of Everest. The team established a route from Darjeeling through the steamy wooded foothills of Sikkim and over into Tibet, becoming the first Europeans to reach Shekar, Tingri and the Rongbuk valley beyond. It was intended as a reconnaissance exercise, and George Mallory and Guy Bullock devoted themselves to looking for a way up Everest and naming some of the surrounding peaks, while other members of the group surveyed the area, took photographs and catalogued the flora and fauna.

From their climbs up Ri Ring and along the Rongbuk and Kangshung glaciers, Mallory and Bullock determined that Everest's West Ridge, North Face and East Face were all too complex and difficult to climb. The North East Ridge looked more promising, although it was not until towards autumn that they climbed up Lhakpa La, and were able to see the East Rongbuk glacier for the first time. They realised that a steep but possible way led from the upper slopes of the glacier onto the North Col, from which there was what looked like a good route to the summit. It was too late in the season to make a proper bid for the top, but mountaineers are always driven to push higher, and on 23rd September 1921 Mallory, Bullock, Wheeler and three porters finally reached the North Col (23,000ft;7,010m).

The Mount Everest Committee sent another expedition the following spring, this time under the leadership of Charles Bruce. There were two attempts on the summit, the first without oxygen, and the second using what the Sherpas called 'English air'. Although the equipment was heavy, cumbersome and unreliable its effects seemed beneficial, with George Finch and Geoffrey Bruce (nephew of Charles Bruce) reaching a record 27,300ft (8,323m). However disaster struck with the third attempt as seven porters climbing up the snow slopes towards the North Col were killed when an avalanche swept them over a cliff and into a crevasse.

In 1924, two years later, Teddy Norton was expedition leader, and Mallory, with his experience from the two previous expeditions, climbing leader. Despite terrible weather the team made two attempts on the summit. Somervell and Norton went first, without oxygen, with Norton reaching 28,126ft (8,575m). That was to remain a record height for a climb without oxygen for 54 years.

Mallory made the second attempt and took Sandy Irvine with him, even though the younger man was still a relatively inexperienced mountaineer compared to some of the others in the team. It seems likely that this choice was partly because of Irvine's skill at tinkering with the temperamental oxygen equipment, for by then Mallory had resolved his initial purist ideals and was convinced that oxygen could help. Perhaps he also recognised that the two of them shared a will to give the summit push every last ounce of energy. Famously, Mallory and Irvine left Camp VI early on 8 June 1924. Noel Odell climbed up towards Camp VI the same morning to try and capture their distant figures with his camera lens, and also to explore the geology of the north face, finding the first fossils on Everest. Although the cloud swirling around the upper slopes of the mountain meant a photograph was impossible, Odell did see two distant figures beneath a rock step in the ridge. He was conscious that they were behind schedule, with only a few hours of daylight left to get up to the summit and back to Camp VI, but was not unduly worried.

He reached Camp VI himself at around 2pm, just as it was starting to snow. He waited there for an hour or so, and then went down to Camp IV, as Mallory had previously instructed. The following day, when Mallory and Irvine had not returned, he climbed back up the mountain, first to Camp V and then to Camp VI. Both were as they had been when he had left. With heavy hearts the men still on the upper slopes laid six blankets out in the shape of a cross on a snow slope at the North Col, signalling to those down at Camp III to abandon hope.

Since then Mallory and Irvine's story has been told and retold. In 1999, seemingly against the odds, George Mallory's body was found and perhaps one day Sandy Irvine's remains will be traced too, or the camera they took with them. Until then what they achieved, and what happened to them, can only be speculation; and despite all the different theories, are still as much of a mystery as they were in 1932 when Maurice Wilson read about the 1924 expedition.

After more loss of life on the mountain the Tibetan authorities opposed further attempts, and the next expedition did not take place until almost ten years later, in 1933. Then Hugh Ruttledge led a new generation of climbers, who had mountaineering experience from different peaks around the world. Maybe this time Everest would be conquered.

Again the team made two attempts on the summit, using a top camp at 27,400ft (8,354m), which was higher than any made previously. Lawrence Wager and Percy Wyn-Harris made the first attempt, and although they were unable to make the second step they did find Irvine's ice axe and managed to climb to over 28,000ft (8,530m). After a couple of days kept back in camp through bad weather, Frank Smythe and Eric Shipton made a second attempt. Shipton found he was struggling and turned back near the First Step. Smythe continued alone, reaching a similar height to Wager and Wyn-Harris before retreating. In one of his books he graphically described his experience of being alone so high on Everest: 'Wherever I looked hostile rocks frowned down on my impotent strugglings, and the wall above seemed almost to overhang me with its dark strata set one upon the other, an embodiment of static, but pitiless, force.'[2]

Although Maurice Wilson was committed to his venture well before Frank Smythe shrank in awe at the might and enormity of Everest, this is what he was to face.

AMBITION AIRBORNE

I learned what every dreaming child needs to know
– that no horizon is so far that you cannot get above
it or beyond it.

Beryl Markham

What had begun as a germ of an idea while Maurice Wilson was in the Black Forest, strengthened and developed in his mind as he journeyed home late in the summer of 1932, and then prepared to settle back into life in England. I imagine it gave him a focus if he feared the black feelings of despair returning to claim him again. Now he had strong faith and a meaningful goal, and with them came boundless positive energy and a fresh lightness of step.

Leonard and Enid Evans were relieved to find their friend cheerful again, and claiming to be fully restored, both mentally and physically. Maurice Wilson was on a high, eager to tell them about his new belief in the purifying and strengthening effects of fasting, his certainty that someone with enough faith could achieve anything, and his dream of demonstrating this publicly by climbing Everest. I wonder what they thought; maybe they even asked themselves if he had lost his mind, rather than working through his depression. Either way I expect they feared the outcome, for the odds were stacked against his quest. But it seems they respected his belief, accepted the challenge he had set himself and supported him as much as they could. Perhaps, faced with his single-minded determination and strength of character, they realised there was little else they could do.

A Gypsy Moth, like 'Ever Wrest'. Photograph courtesy of the de Havilland Aircraft Museum.

Having chosen to climb Everest, it is not so surprising that Maurice Wilson came up with the idea of flying to the base of the mountain. As wealth and confidence had increased in the years after the First World War, the romance of flying grew. People saw the skies as a new, hopeful and exciting frontier. Year by year men and women flew within days to distant and exotic countries that generally took journeys of months by sea, some finding fame, if not fortune, in the process. The world of flying was a thrilling but perilous mix of the intrepid and the informal, with daring aviators improvising landing places, spare parts and navigation. John Alcock and Arthur Brown successfully crossed the Atlantic in 1919, despite having to reach out in mid air and use their hands and a penknife to clear ice from the two engines of their Vickers Vimy; Sir Alan Cobham flew to Australia and back in 1926, establishing a route over the Middle East and India; in 1928 Charles Kingford-Smith flew across the Pacific to Australia and by 1932 people like Jim Mollison, Amy Johnson, Amelia Earhart and Charles Lindbergh were international celebrities.

By the time Maurice Wilson returned to London, small bi-planes were regularly seen over the city, and passengers sat on the open top deck of buses running along the Edgware Road had a good view of both the aircraft and their leather helmeted pilots as they glided in to land at the north London aerodrome. Maurice Wilson had seen enough in France to know what a pilot could do with his craft. And now aero-planes were taking off from rough grass and earth airstrips all over the world, their pilots often landing them on any avail-able piece of ground – so why not on the lower slopes of Everest? It would attract public attention straightaway. And for someone wanting to reach the mountain's summit it would also save the long, arduous march from Darjeeling.

In the UK, more and more people wanted to taste the glam-our and excitement of flying, and clubs were set up all over the country. The government was keen to promote aviation, anxious to maintain the country's influential position in a fast changing world, and gave financial support to five of them, administered through the Royal Aero Club. This meant sub-sidised flying lessons were available in London, Durham, Lancashire, the Midlands and Scotland, although learning to fly was still a costly undertaking. The London Aeroplane Club at Stag Lane near Hendon was well known, with a wait-ing list of those wanting to join. As Amy Johnson had done four years before him, Maurice Wilson applied to be elected as an associate member.

By 1932, the Stag Lane airfield was busy and popular. There were streets of suburban houses surprisingly close, and the de Havilland Aircraft Company works alongside. Visitors who ignored the large notice reading 'London Aeroplane Club: Private' found a runway, a roughly level grassed area, four adjoining hangars and a wooden clubhouse with deck chairs set out on its veranda for members and their guests to watch the flying machines take off and land, and share their tales of past exploits. It was noisy, sometimes cold and, as aeroplanes came and went, the air reeked of petrol and engine oil – but, I imagine, it felt a fresh, innovative and passionate place to be.

Once his plan had taken shape, Maurice Wilson began to prepare with enthusiasm and commitment. With confident determination, he bought himself an aeroplane before he had even begun his flying lessons. After some thought he settled on a de Havilland Gypsy Moth, buying a second hand 1930 Gypsy II with the serial letters G-ABJC. The Gypsy Moth was a good choice; having been first introduced in 1925 with a reliable 100hp Cirrus engine, it was tried and tested, and was used both by flying schools and for record-breaking long distance flights. With a solid wooden frame, fixed undercarriage and cloth-covered wings, it had a wing span of 29ft 8in (9.1m), a length of 23ft 11in (7.3m) and, although its top speed was 102mph (164kph), it could comfortably manage a cruising speed of 85mph (136kph). While learning to fly was simply a means to an end for Maurice Wilson, he had enough feeling for his purchase to name her, carefully painting *Ever Wrest* on the nose cone.

Amy Johnson used a 1928 Gypsy Moth, which she called Jason (G-AAAH), for her solo flight from England to Australia in 1930. Afterwards she gave it to the British people, who so idolised and feted her, and it now hangs in the Science Museum in London, like a life size Airfix model. In our health and safety conscious modern world it seems difficult to appreciate how people gambled their lives against the elements in such light and fragile looking things. In the early

Maurice Wilson, the airman.

21st century, most of us see flying as basically safe. In 1932, many of the tiny minority who took to the skies did not expect to see old age – and to those with 'the bug', flying brought a massive adrenaline rush of excitement and danger.

※ ※ ※ ※ ※ ※ ※

At last Maurice Wilson had his first lesson. Beginning on the ground, the then chief flying instructor at Stag Lane, Nigel Tangye, explained the rudimentary instruments of the flying club's dual control Moth – compass, rev counter, altimeter, air speed, oil pressure and temperature gauges and throttle – and showed him how to use a windsock to check wind direction and speed. Then, dressed in thick leather jackets, helmets, heavy gloves and goggles, they clambered into the two small open cockpits – instructor in the front and his pupil behind. Nigel Tangye took the aircraft down the runway facing into the wind, slowly at first but gathering pace, and then gently eased the throttle until they were airborne.

Looking out over the side, below shoulder height for a man as tall as he was, Maurice Wilson could see their movement along the ground as the grass beside the runway seemed to slip away from them. Momentarily his feelings took hold, and in a sudden wave of panic, the wood and cloth structure of the Moth felt too flimsy to survive in the enormity of the sky. The overpowering smells of oil, petrol and tar filled his nose and throat, his ears were almost deafened by the noise of the engine and the throb of the exhaust and, with his head feeling it was about to explode, he was sure he would never remember all the things he had been told. Then, realising the wheels had left the ground, his stomach lurched and his throat tightened, but as the machine roared they rose steadily, first over the aerodrome fence, then over back gardens and at last above the rows of Hendon rooftops. Ahead lay the sprawling mass of the capital – from the air a toy town of miniature

roads, brick houses, factories, red buses, and a few cars all
dissected by the dark kinking line of the Thames. As Maurice
Wilson leant forward, trying to settle his mind by picking out
the city's landmarks, his instructor banked steeply round and
headed north until they were over open fields.

Now it was Maurice Wilson's turn. As Nigel Tangye bel-
lowed instructions through a speaking tube, which connected
from the instructor's cockpit to an earpiece in the pupil's helmet, he tried out the Moth's two main controls; the joystick
and the foot operated rudder bar. Holding the joystick light-
ly he was told to gently follow the movements Nigel Tangye
made on the instructor's dual controls, and to feel how they
altered the aeroplane's pitch, and then to do the same with his
feet to sense the effects of rudder movements on the yaw of
the Moth. This exercise was intended to show pupils how to
gain and lose height, how to bank and turn, and how to keep
the aircraft on an even keel; and each needed smooth, gentle
but confident movements to keep the aeroplane from jerking
and see-sawing. Sensing just how much to move hands and
feet to keep the Moth flying smoothly came to some people
with intuition and instinct, but for other novices needed hard
work and persistence.

Like learning to drive, learning to fly is an intensely personal experience, and I imagine this was even more so in
those uncomputerised early decades. First perhaps a thrill of
anticipation, or a sense of the strangeness of the aeroplane
with its smells and sounds; then an ordeal of confusion and
fear, followed by frustration, helplessness and impatience as
skills mastered one day seem to turn to ham-fisted failure the
next; then maybe, exhilaration, triumph and satisfaction – and
last, the understanding and acceptance of new 'mug' pilots
that however well things go there is always more to learn.

As an airman it seems Maurice Wilson was not a natural;
instinct did not give him an easy communication with his
machine, nor a sense of how to adapt to weather conditions.

Lesson after lesson Nigel Tangye reminded him to keep his movements slow and smooth. I imagine his pupil cursing and muttering under his breath, gritting his teeth, thinking of Everest and trying again, working to co-ordinate his hands and feet, to keep his eyes on the instruments, to watch the horizon and feel the wind, and to learn to look below him for landmarks – rivers, railways, canals and the wide Edgware Road, which was his route back to the airfield. With grim determination he stuck at it, and Nigel Tangye perhaps began to realise that Maurice Wilson had strengths to help him succeed where others might well have given up.

Trying to build up his flying experience over the winter months brought the additional frustration of unpredictable weather. Not only did it make the open cockpits bitterly cold, but the low lying Stag Lane airfield was prone to mist and fog, meaning lesson times were uncertain, and if the smog was particularly bad could be cancelled for several days. Aspiring pilots had to kick their heels around the hangars and clubhouse, smoking, drinking mugs of tea, watching the mechanics at work and waiting for the clinging cloud to lift.

Maurice Wilson was not the only person to find learning to fly time consuming and aggravatingly less straightforward than it looked. Sir Francis Chichester described himself as 'a slow pupil',[1] and with the average time for pilots to get their A licences (allowing them to fly solo) being eight to twelve hours, Amy Johnson took 15 hours 45 minutes. Maurice Wilson flew with Nigel Tangye for just over nineteen hours before, in February 1933, he was allowed to take *Ever Wrest* up on his own. It must have been an exciting moment, and I imagine he was quietly satisfied with his achievement.

When he first dreamed of Everest, Maurice Wilson could neither fly nor climb – now he owned an aeroplane and was a qualified pilot. However he was wise enough to realise that there was a big difference between holding his A licence and being fully competent. He practiced regularly to build up his flying hours, taking *Ever Wrest* out over London whenever he had chance, moving to lodgings nearer the airfield and flying from there most mornings.

That winter he also devoted as much time as he could to getting fit. Since his return from the Black Forest Maurice Wilson had fasted regularly for eight to ten days at a stretch, believing that it would be good preparation for the rigours of his coming journey. Although I doubt this would stand up to scientific scrutiny, he spoke of his theory that the sun burned the oxygen out of the air at high altitudes. To combat this he planned to climb in the early morning and late evening, and to only eat one meal a day to help him take in more oxygen.

Stag Lane had become as much of a second home as the Evans's suburban house and so he often exercised by marching around and around the perimeter fence of the airfield, which I imagine will have either bemused or entertained his fellow club members. Although this was a far cry from the Himalayas, he made several journeys to Bradford to see his mother and brothers, walking the 200 mile distance between London and Yorkshire's West Riding in five or six days to increase his stamina. And in the early months of 1933 he spent five weeks in the Lake District and the Welsh mountains to try and get used to hiking up steep slopes, periodically with snow, and scrambling over rocks. At the same time, *Ever Wrest* was taken into the de Havilland workshop for some special modifications – extra fuel tanks along with a heavier and stronger undercarriage.

During the companionable and comfortable evenings he spent with the Evanses they together planned his route to India, calculated where he could land for fuel and worked out what equipment he should carry with him, both out to the Himalayas by air and then up the mountain. Maurice Wilson engaged the Automobile Association to apply for the necessary flight permits, and arrange for fuel, oil and maintenance work to be available at a series of scheduled stopping points.

He was forced to keep his luggage to a minimum. Although *Ever Wrest* could carry two people, the amount of extra fuel meant that everything else had to be restricted to what was essential – some clothes, his boots, a tent, sleeping bag, height recorder, oxygen equipment, his camera, a Union Jack to raise on the summit and his personal 'flag of friendship', a silk pennant signed by friends and well wishers, and lastly supplies for his flight. His oxygen equipment alone weighed 18lb (8.16kg), but he had been told it would give enough to last seven and a half hours, and as most of the previous Everest expedition members seemed to agree that oxygen could help, he packed it carefully.

By 1933, there was sufficient international air travel for a chain of airports to have evolved, and the developing commercial passenger flights added to the private civil traffic. Through the 1919 International Air Convention, most countries agreed to allow the aircraft of other nations to fly over their territory, notable exceptions being what was then Persia's refusal to allow Britain's Imperial Airways overflight and landing rights, and Nepal and Tibet's exclusion of all aircraft. During the 1920s, European national airlines had emerged, including Air France, KLM, Sabena and Lufthansa, and, in the UK, Imperial Airlines (known as Imps in the flying fraternity). Although the ambitious British plans for airships had ended with the 1930 R101 tragedy, Germany was still committed to its airship programme at the time, providing luxury lounges, bedrooms and social areas for passengers. The fuel companies developed their own networks to supply the airports and support the intrepid pilots who trusted their lives to the air, although facilities on the ground were often rough and ready, and many did not have garage style pumps. Sir Francis Chichester later wrote that it was almost always a

problem to get oil and petrol. Shell were particularly successful, providing information on aerodromes, weather conditions and routes, as well as offering a prepaid carnet service
for customers to finance their fuel, and even servicing work,
around the world before leaving the UK.

Through the Automobile Association, an official notice of
Maurice Wilson's intention to fly to Purnea, in north-east
India, and then back to Britain, was sent in March 1933, and
the necessary permission from the British and Indian authorities was given without difficulty. At this point it is impossible to know whether he simply never considered the need to
get approval to fly on from Purnea or if he deliberately
ignored it, and relied on keeping his intentions sufficiently
secret from the authorities until he was over the border and
into Nepal. However, as his scheduled date for leaving
England neared Maurice Wilson was persuaded to tell the
press his plans. Given his aim of showing the world the
power and inspiration of his faith, he embraced this suggestion enthusiastically. Not surprisingly the press loved both
him and his story.

At the time the British public was fired up with the idea of
flying to Everest, as the success of the Houston-Westland
expedition meant the world was celebrating man's first flight
over the mountain. On 3 April 1933, Lord Clydesdale,
Colonel Blacker, Flight Lieutenant McIntyre and the camera-
man S R Bonnett took off from Purnea and managed to fly
two specially modified Westland bi-planes over Everest's
summit, clearing it by just 100ft (30m) as their planes were
battered with icy fragments from the mountain's famous
snow plume. They recorded their achievement with some
magnificent photographs, and Everest's sharp rock slopes and
glaciers stood out from the front pages of newspapers.

Although the Houston-Westland triumph meant that the
timing of Maurice Wilson sharing his story with the press was
ideal for catching newspaper readers' imaginations, this early

exposure also brought unwelcome publicity to an embarrassing incident. Having flown north to say goodbye to his mother, and to get used to piloting *Ever Wrest* again after her modifications, he was forced to crash land in a field near Cleckheaton (in Yorkshire), hitting a tree before he tipped and skidded to an inelegant halt against a hedge, having to be rescued from the cockpit by a passing schoolboy. Although Maurice Wilson was unhurt, his Gypsy Moth was badly damaged, and had to be transported back to London for three weeks of repairs. As he had intended to leave on 21 April, his birthday, this was a bitter disappointment.

However he was undaunted, and continued to appear both positive and cheerful. On 25 April one of the newspapers reported an interview with him. 'Stop me? They haven't a dog's chance,' said Mr Wilson to the *Daily Sketch* yesterday. 'I am as determined on this flight as anyone who ever undertook a record flight. I've been eight months studying the mountains. I have spent two months in an aeroplane, and I am as well equipped as it is possible to be. Am I going to give up all my efforts just because of a minor accident in England? No. Not for all the expert views ever advanced.'[2]

More seriously the Civil Aviation Authority was alerted, partly by the newspaper reports but also following a letter sent to the director of their India office by a Mr L V Heathcote of the Burmah-Shell Oil Storage and Distributing Company of India. This explained he had been warned by the company's London office that Maurice Wilson's plan was to fly not only to Purnea, but on from there over the border into Nepal, and to land on Everest. 'I am not at all sure that it is any business of ours,' he continued, 'but do you think that to allow such a suicidal journey to be undertaken is going to do civil aviation any good?' He asked, 'have you powers to stop the attempt and if you have, would you think of exercising them?'[3] offering to let the Authority know should *Ever Wrest* land in Karachi.

Consequently, on 8 May 1933 the Authority's deputy
director in London wrote to Maurice Wilson asking whether
there was any foundation to the press reports that he intended to go beyond his official destination. This letter went on
to explain both that he would not be able to fly to Everest
from Purnea without the consent of the government of Nepal,
and that it was doubtful whether any such permission would
be forthcoming. In his rather high-handed reply Maurice
Wilson pointed out that the Houston-Westland expedition had
flown from India to Everest, just as he intended to do. In his
concluding paragraph he commented waspishly, 'If it is the
desire of the Air Ministry to foster the development of civil
aviation, I would suggest that an offer of assistance would
have been the more correct, and sporting, attitude for you to
have taken up.'[4] Rather oddly he then added, 'Without prej-
udice,' before signing. (Although it shows very clearly how
he felt at the time, he later conceded in a letter to a friend in
England that it had perhaps been foolish! It was certainly not
the most measured or diplomatic approach he could have
taken.)

The Civil Aviation Authority countered this response by
explaining that the Nepalese government had agreed to the
Houston-Westland flight, but only after careful negotiations
and in return for certain undertakings. The letter warned that
he would not be allowed to fly over the border without the
Nepalese government's consent, and that the Authority therefore could not encourage a flight to Everest which would
involve crossing Nepalese territory. Maurice Wilson ignored
it.

Finally the Authority sent him a telegram. 'Indian government state they are not prepared to approach Nepal government for permission for your flight to Everest, and desire you
to be warned that in no circumstances will you be permitted
to make the attempt.'[5] Maurice Wilson viewed this in much
the same light as he had his accident near Cleckheaton. 'Stop

me? They haven't a dog's chance' became something of a mantra for his journey.

Maurice Wilson left Stag Lane for his ambitious flight to India on the morning of Sunday 21 May 1933, with reporters, friends and well-wishers there to see him off, including his faithful confidants Enid and Leonard Evans. At least some of them must have thought they could be saying good-bye for the last time. 'I have pointed out the risks he is running, but he is determined to see it through,'[6] Nigel Tangye told the *Sunday Pictorial*. I wonder what the outwardly cheery Maurice Wilson felt. Even if he admitted any misgivings or second thoughts to himself, I cannot believe he would have shared them. He does not seem to have been a man who acknowledged his feelings much. He was brave, he believed he had been chosen for this mission, and he had an important job to do – any fear was held deep inside. But I hope at least he had a stomach turning thrill of anticipation at finally being on his way to Everest.

Having cleared customs at Heston airport in Middlesex, it seems appropriate that he flew first to Freiburg in Germany, where he spent the late afternoon and evening visiting old haunts and acquaintances. Up early the following morning he made the short hop to Passau, intending to fly over the Alps, but was forced by bad weather to change direction. As the press and his friends speculated and worried in turn about where he might be, he worked out a route over Lake Geneva to Marseilles and on to Italy, stopping at Pisa, where he was welcomed as a hero, followed by Rome and Naples. He grew used to long hours listening to the steady sound of the engine, to solitude in the sky with Europe stretched out below him, and to the sensation of time and distance slipping past *Ever Wrest's* wing tips.

At each stopping point there was a colourful hubbub of excitement and activity. He had to show his papers and permits to a wearying succession of customs and immigration officials, and deal as patiently as he could with question after question. Then he flew over the bright blue Mediterranean to Tunisia, where he had his first brush with the local police and resorted to refuelling *Ever Wrest* himself from a pile of rusty looking canisters. Lifting and tipping each can by hand, he had to filter both oil and petrol through a chamois leather to try and prevent any particles of rust or dirt getting into the engine and clogging the carburettor jets, something that could have been enough to force a landing. The Gypsy Moth had no petrol gauge, and the only way to tell whether her fuel tanks were full was by reaching his finger inside them.

Not far from the Lybian border the plane developed engine trouble. Fortunately Maurice Wilson was able to get to the desert airstrip of Gabes before it cut out – there had been water in the fuel. From there he flew along the barren North African coast in fairly short stages. Although the weather was good, the rough air above the coast produced pockets of turbulence, and *Ever Wrest* was tossed about alarmingly, each bump showering petrol into the cockpit from the open fuel tanks, while Maurice Wilson strained his eyes against the glare of the sun and looked for landmarks in the featureless miles of rocks and sand below. He stopped at Tripoli, Benghazi, Tobruk, Sidi Barrani, Alexandria and finally Cairo, appreciating the easy route of the Nile and the soft green relief of vegetation on either side of it. He landed at the Egyptian capital a week after leaving Stag Lane and satisfyingly bang on schedule. He was tired and ready for a good meal and a hot bath, his face was burnt and sore from the Mediterranean sun, his lips were split, he could taste petrol in his throat, he was spattered with fuel and oil, and it felt as though the roar of *Ever Wrest's* engine and the throb of her exhaust had drummed into every nerve of his body, but he

TO FLY ALONE OVER EVEREST

MR. MAURICE WILSON, aged thirty-five, of Shipley, Bradford, left London alone in his airplane yesterday to fly to Mount Everest, where he will attempt to land and plant the Union Jack on the summit. He hopes to climb the last 15,000 feet on foot. He learned to fly only in February.

Maurice Wilson leaving London.

grinned cheerfully and confidently.

Unfortunately, it was while he was in Egypt that his plans started to go wrong. Before he had left London he understood, presumably through the Automobile Association, that his permission to fly through Persia had been granted, and would be waiting for him in Cairo. He contacted the British RAF officials when he arrived, but 'registered immediately there was nothing doing'[7] and was told there was no permit for him. Having left the airport mechanics to give *Ever Wrest* a thorough service, he tried different telephone numbers, different offices and different officials but, with increasing frustration, got nowhere. I imagine the warning from the Civil Aviation Authority echoed sickeningly in his ears. The British authorities had long arms. But, squaring his shoulders, he managed to fight weary despondency and faceless officialdom with grim resolution. If his destiny was to climb Everest; his journey could not end with the Sphinx and the pyramids.

'Well Everest wasn't Cairo,' he wrote later, 'so on I pushed to Bagdhad.'[8] He made the roughly 1,000 mile (1,609km) journey in a day, calling at Suez, Gaza, Bethlehem and Gadda. For a still relatively inexperienced pilot this was a big undertaking. It was fiercely hot and *Ever Wrest* rocked and swung about in turbulence above the desert. The landscape was bleak and monotonous, mile after mile of grey brown sand with jagged rocky outcrops, and occasionally a line of camels or a group of nomads' tents. Screwing up his eyes against the sun, he had to concentrate hard to spot places on the ground that corresponded with his map, using his compass and trusting to faith. He felt sick with the heat, his head ached, and folded up in the cramped cockpit his broad frame was numb; fighting terrible sleepiness he squirmed in his seat desperately trying to find a new part of his body to sit on. It must have been an immense relief to see Bagdhad. The city was visible from miles away, and the modern, well-appointed airfield, set apart from the maze of mosques, markets and narrow streets, was easy to spot. Circling, he weighed up the best place to bring *Ever Wrest* down, before landing on the grass and beaten earth runway, and thankfully but shakily climbing down onto solid ground. There was only about half an hour to sunset.

Although Britain's League of Nations mandate over Iraq had officially ended in 1932, there was still a strong British military peacekeeping presence in the country, including involvement by the RAF. Maurice Wilson asked again about his permit to fly over Persia, only for a succession of officials to give the same responses he had heard in Cairo. Any permit there had been could not be found. He tried to apply for a new one, but was told it was out of the question. If he landed in Persia, even if it was just to refuel, he would be arrested. The government was determined that British interests and influence in both the Middle East and the Indian subcontinent would not be prejudiced or embarrassed by the actions of one eccentric citizen. However, following a friendlier and more fruitful conversation with some RAF pilots and crewmen, Maurice Wilson decided that the solution was to change his plans and avoid Persia altogether.

From this brief debate, he realised there was an alternative route around the southern side of the Persian Gulf through Bahrain, which was then a British protectorate and a stopping off point for the Imperial Airways flights that were banned from Persia. From there he could follow the coast to Sharjah and Muscat. He managed to buy a map in Bagdhad but it only showed half the area, and he needed to tackle the roughly 700 mile (1,125km) journey to Bahrain in one go. Even with the additional fuel tanks that had been added before he left London, this was very close to his Gypsy Moth's maximum range.

After tossing and turning through what must have been a stifling and uncertain night, he left Bagdhad shortly after dawn the following morning. He calculated that the journey should take him roughly nine hours. The first half of the flight was much like his previous day had been – dull and uncomfortable hours trying to steady *Ever Wrest* through bumpy air over endless sand that seemed to run from horizon to horizon, while the sun beat into his face, trickles of sweat made their way down his neck and back, and his throat burned as dry as sandpaper with thirst. Basra was easy to recognise from the wide belts of date palms growing on either side of the Tigris, and by then he could just see the glittering blue of the Persian Gulf beyond an expanse of swampy land that led to the estuary.

Once beyond the coast there would be no more need to worry about Iraq's infamous bandits, who regarded all aircraft as belonging to the RAF, and so tended to fire

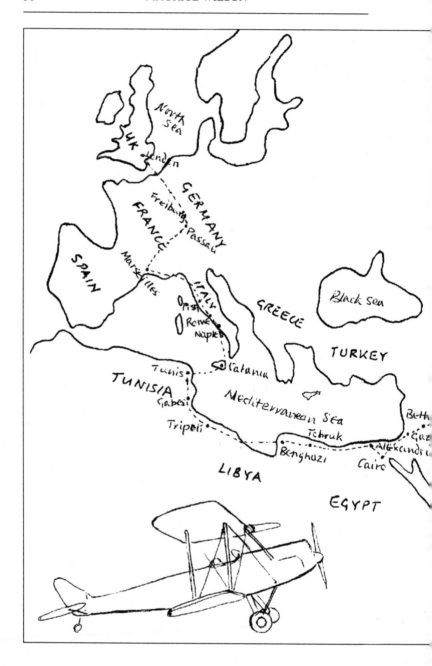

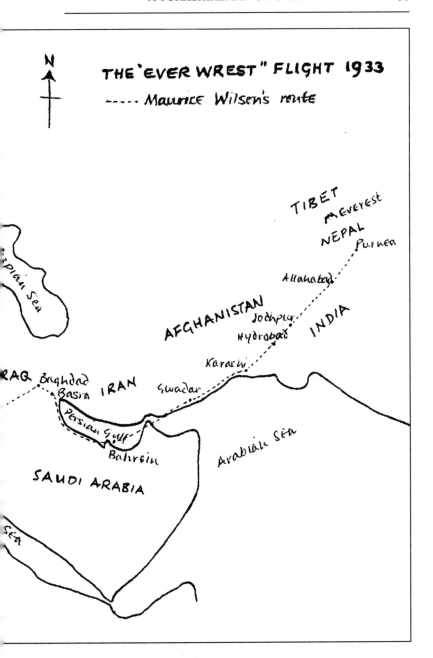

indiscriminately at passing planes, but instead Maurice Wilson knew that if he either ran out of fuel or had problems with the engine there was no chance of making a forced landing. Suspended in his fragile machine, isolation above the sea must have seemed even more exposed than isolation over the desert.

A thick, shimmering haze hanging above the Gulf meant a rocky ride, and I imagine that the heat and blistering sun made it feel like flying through an endless inferno. Increasing height helped a little. Breathing petrol fumes I guess Maurice Wilson could hardly remember what cool fresh air was. He could not be bothered with his snacks of dates, raisins and nuts. However much he shuffled round in his seat, his body was either numb or tormented by pins and needles, and he battled an immobilising and dangerous weariness. Normally the long task of hand pumping fuel from the fuselage tanks to the gravity operated top wing tank was a chore, but in those sapping hours of tedium it became a welcome relief, and he was even glad to focus on the protesting pain of his biceps as he worked.

At his first distant sight of Bahrain, Maurice Wilson must have wondered whether it was a mirage, or a trick of his mind, but as he kept *Ever Wrest* on her course what had been a faint shadow grew more solid and gradually came closer. He landed on the new airstrip and crawled out from his seat, while one of the mechanics hurried to help him. Even on the ground there was no respite from the day's heat, and the air smelt of oil and sand, but at least he had made it. Stiffly, with his head thumping and his eyes half closed from hours of squinting, he pushed chocks under *Ever Wrest's* wheels and headed for the airport building to arrange for his fuel tanks to be filled, and to book a bath, refreshments and a bed for the night.

Apologetically, the airport officials explained that Bahrain's British Political Agent had given strict instructions that he was not to be allowed any petrol. It must have been a desperate moment; since he had reached Egypt the authorities always seemed to have been a step ahead. Summoning all his patience, and forcing the weariness from his face with a smile of urbane innocence, he accompanied one of the Imperial Airways staff to meet the Political Agent, Lt Col Gordon Loch. Maurice Wilson explained that he had not flown over Persia and did not plan to do so, as his intention was to go to Sharjah, and then on to Gwadar, in India, from there. Consequently, he cajoled, there was no need for the prohibition on fuel. However, following an exchange of telegrams with RAF Headquarters, the Political Agent explained that he could not travel on to Sharjah and along the Arabian coast, the only civil aircraft allowed that way being Imperial Airways commercial flights. I imagine he was seething inwardly, but Maurice Wilson agreed to reflect overnight on two options – whether to risk flying north over the Gulf to Bushire, in Persia, and to ask for a permit there, which carried the risk of arrest by local police, or to undertake the exhausting nine hour journey back to Bagdhad.

When I first heard about it, this was one of my highlights from Maurice Wilson's journey; it reads like a chapter of a school child's adventure book. He decided to 'bluff'. The following morning, scrubbed and clean, he presented himself at the Political Agent's office and said that he had decided returning to Bagdhad was his best choice. He asked for permission to refuel, and this time his request was granted.

Afterwards he told the story in a letter back to England. 'There was a map in the vestibule and while he was inside writing out my fuel permit I roughed out the distance to Gwadar, *the next stop on my forward route to India,* and took the scale of the map on my coat sleeve.

'Later I worked out that my tankage (with the extra fuel obtained on the new permit) would leave me thirty miles to spare, that was if my gamble on fine weather came off. With

that I stuck an additional four gallon tin of petrol in my front
locker, filled up my tanks and took off. To make short of a
long story I was nine and a half hours in the air, nine hours
out of landing distance and five hours without sight of land.
My rev counter suddenly went bung, the indicator flew back
to zero and I had a momentary hustle for my life belt, but I
landed at Gwadar safely ten minutes before dark, with petrol
on the nod to extinction.'[9]

Gordon Loch's formal report to the Political Resident for
the Persian Gulf area makes less dramatic, but perhaps more
balanced, reading. When Maurice Wilson first came to see
him, on the afternoon of 31 May 1933, he formed the view
that the English airman had come to Bahrain 'in good faith',
particularly as he 'expressed regret' for having done so if it
was out of bounds. The report continued, 'I was not clear to
what extent responsibility for his appearance in Bahrain and
his consequent difficulties lay in fact with him.' Gordon
Loch then explained that he had allowed *Ever Wrest* to be
refuelled the following day. 'Mr Wilson undertook to return
to Basrah (and I think genuinely intended to do so), but eventually landed at Gwadar. The Agent of Imperial Airways and
I agree, however, that the wind, which greatly increased in
velocity not long after he had taken off, would have rendered
it almost impossible for the Moth to have made Basrah.'[10]

After *Ever Wrest* had left, Gordon Loch sent telegrams to
the airports at Sharjah and Gwadar stipulating that if Maurice
Wilson landed he was not to be allowed to refuel without his
authority. Shortly afterwards the message to Gwadar was
cancelled when the Political Agent himself received a
telegram confirming there was no objection to Maurice
Wilson landing at Gwadar, given the permission he already
had to fly to Purnea.

Official correspondence around Maurice Wilson's flight
also shows that the British authorities' objection to his alternative route was not a personal one. A note, dated 15 July

1933, observed, 'the Air Ministry might be informed of what has happened and might ask the recognised agents in this country – AA, RAC, etc. – to impress upon their clients that the Arab route is out of bounds.' Its author added, unexpectedly flippantly in a government paper, '(You may remember that the Admiralty thought we could leave its protection to the sharks.)'![(11)]

Whether Maurice Wilson's route was inspired by bluff and planned on his coat sleeve, or was dictated by the weather, in one exhausting day he had crossed the Persian Gulf, the Gulf of Oman and part of the Arabian Sea; but at last he was in India. I imagine him bringing *Ever Wrest* down towards the coast, gradually losing height, the engine spluttering and unsteady on the last of its fuel, seeing trees and fields ahead, and grinning to himself through a dizzy veil of tiredness – 'Stop me? They haven't a dog's chance'.

MARKING TIME

*All men dream: but not equally. Those who dream
by night in the dusty recesses of their mind wake in
the day to find that it was vanity: but the dreamers
of the day are dangerous men, for they may act
their dream with open eyes, to make it possible.*

T E Lawrence

Physically and mentally spent, Maurice Wilson slowly and
painfully pulled himself up to the rim of *Ever Wrest's* cockpit
and dropped heavily onto the ground. Somehow, he had
made it. As if the unfamiliar silence was too much to cope
with, his head continued to throb with engine noise. Almost
in a daze he lent back against the plane, struggling to straight-
en his body, and watched the sun set far away over the
Arabian Sea, a brilliant fireball colouring both the darkening
sky and the inky sea with orange, scarlet and purple. Then,
as dusk moved quickly to a deep, black darkness, the cue for
the night-time insects to start their chorus and for hundreds of
bats to fly from their roosts, he curled up in his sleeping bag
next to the dependable Gypsy Moth. His head ached and his
body still felt to be moving, but he was too tired for either that
or his strange surroundings to keep him awake long.

The following morning, after 'a wonderful night under
starlit skies'[1], he refuelled and then began his journey across
pre-partition India. Exhausted by his marathon days of flying, his reserves depleted by the heat, and with his eyes red
and sore from long hours of concentrating in bright sunlight,
Maurice Wilson allowed himself the luxury of travelling in

Maurice Wilson was still an inexperienced pilot when he left for his solo flight to India.

easy stages, taking roughly a week over it. First Karachi, then Hyderabad, Jodhpur, Allahabad, and finally following the sacred Ganges to Purnea. Ominously he was twice refused petrol on the orders of the British authorities, but both times managed to find an alternative supply.

He was full of optimism. Not only had he completed the flight, but he also seemed to have overcome the obstacles the government had thrown at him. It showed God really was with him; and that all he needed was faith.

While he was in Karachi he spoke to the *Daily Express* correspondent, and the newspaper ran its story on 9 June 1933 reporting that Maurice Wilson was 'completing preparations for his attempt.'

'Enough rice and dates to last fifty days will be in my rucksack when I begin to climb Mount Everest after landing on the mountain 10,000 ft up,' he said. 'One fit, trained man can succeed where a large group will fail.'

Mr Wilson reckons that eight days will be required for the foot climb up and down. 'For ten months I have trained,' he said, 'testing foods and special fasts, until I have found that the best procedure is to take one meal a day, which will enable me to breathe down to my stomach, taking in a vastly increased supply of oxygen.'

His ten months of training and experimenting have given him the utmost confidence. He considers his optimism fully justified, as he has read every book and studied every map of Everest in that period. 'There is no stunt about it,' he reiterated. 'It is a carefully planned expedition, which is certain of success, although the orthodox minded may consider it madness.' [2]

Maurice Wilson's plan was to spend a couple of days in Purnea, resting and organising his equipment and food supplies, before flying on to the lower slopes of Everest and taking pot luck, landing the Gypsy Moth where he could and then striking for the top from there.

Unfortunately the authorities still had other ideas. As the Civil Aviation Authority explained in the correspondence before he left England, the Indian government had helped the Houston-Westland expedition get permission from the Maharaja for their flight over Nepal, but were not prepared to either endorse Maurice Wilson's unofficial attempt or risk their quiet but uncontentious relationship with the Nepali government by doing the same again. The Maharaja's consent the previous year had very much been a one off. Neither Nepal nor Tibet wanted contact with the world beyond the Himalayas; the rulers of both countries felt the anger of the mountain gods would be provoked if their peace was disturbed by flying machines, and also recognised on a practical level that men in aeroplanes could mean strangers looking for routes along which invading armies might later march.

While Maurice Wilson was making his way across India, the Foreign Office in Simla exchanged several telegrams with the British Envoy in Nepal, warning the latter of his progress. This exchange explained that the British authorities were 'doing everything possible to dissuade Wilson,' and expressed the view that his planned landing on Everest was doomed to fail. The telegram observed, 'There is however no law to prevent anyone making such attempt from Indian soil but government of India feel that their hands would be strengthened if they could inform Wilson that Nepal government had definitely refused to allow him to cross border.'[3] Not surprisingly, the requested official refusal was given.

As Maurice Wilson saw it, at Purnea 'officialdom won'.[4] He arrived there on 8 June. The following morning the chief of police and local magistrate visited him, and taking the view that he was still determined to fly to Nepal, politely, but firmly, served him with a formal notice preventing him from flying further. Worse, they took his plane and, ignominiously after her historic journey, *Ever Wrest* was put into an open compound under police guard.

The *Standard* printed a brief article: 'He is still hoping to receive permission from the Nepal authorities to fly in the region of Mount Everest,' it explained. 'If this is delayed, Mr Wilson is thinking of making for Kathmandu, but if permission for the flight is refused, he is still determined that he will visit Mount Everest on foot.' [5]

Maurice Wilson spent several frustrating days in Purnea, lurching between energetic anger and crippling low spirits, and fretting over the Gypsy Moth's delicate structure exposed to the humid Indian weather. Getting nowhere with the British Indian authorities he decided to travel overland to Raxaul, which is not far from the Nepal border, and catch a train to Kathmandu to seek permission himself to fly to Everest. The Foreign Office at Simla asked local government officials there to explain that formal agreement would be needed before he could cross into Nepal. Despite this Maurice Wilson was able to travel overland to Birgang, just within the forbidden territory, and then telephoned to Kathmandu to try and arrange a meeting with the Maharaja. This request was refused, and he was told in no uncertain terms to leave Nepal.

Finally Maurice Wilson gave his word that he would not take *Ever Wrest* out of India, and was reunited with his plane. But by then it was July. The monsoon had arrived and, with it, any hope of him attempting Everest in 1933 had gone, for the warm seasonal winds make the snow slopes unstable and dangerous. He was stuck. His only comfort was that Ruttledge's official expedition to the mountain had been forced to turn back in the face of appalling weather. Everest remained unconquered. He could still be the first.

Maurice Wilson had been invited to visit a Major Kent at his plantation at Purtabpore, which was roughly 250 miles (402km) from Purnea, and decided to go as soon as his plane was released from the police compound. But *Ever Wrest* refused to start. 'Couldn't get a kick out of the engine after being so long in alternate rain and sunshine.' However, Maurice Wilson was as patient and resourceful as he was determined. Watched by a curious audience of children and local police officers jostling, chattering together, and pointing, he got out his tools and instruction book, and painstakingly stripped the engine, then cleaned, oiled and reassembled it. Five hours later he 'had the thing running and giving better 'revs' than it had ever done.'[6] The next day he tackled the plane's frame, carefully following the rigging instruction booklet, until he was finally satisfied that *Ever Wrest* would take off safely from the short, wet runway.

Although Maurice Wilson spent some time with Major Kent, his small plantation airstrip had no hangar, and so the Gypsy Moth was still at the mercy of the elements. He took off again, heading for Lucknow. But before reaching the town, and with his fuel supply dropping, he was caught by thick monsoon cloud. He had to fly as low as he could to avoid being bumped too violently in the erratic turbulence, while the rain stung his forehead, streamed into his eyes and ran down his chest and back. Even for someone with Maurice Wilson's courage being tossed about in an open plane in such unpredictable conditions must have been frightening. He needed to find somewhere to land.

Fortunately he spotted an estate at Moniara, Behar, which had its own airstrip laid out on a polo ground, and he was able to bring *Ever Wrest* down safely there. But the weather meant it was neither safe nor wise to continue. Apparently unperturbed by an unexpected visitor, the plantation owner, Cassells, invited Maurice Wilson to stay as his guest until the flying conditions improved. From a letter Maurice Wilson sent to England later, over the following week the two became firm friends, spending many hours talking over tea on the veranda, tramping round the estate and pouring over maps. By then Maurice Wilson had accepted that he could not fly to Everest without the agreement of the authorities, and this meant *Ever Wrest* was of no further use to him. Worse, she was a costly liability as his own funds were running low, and she was deteriorating rapidly stood outside in the damp, humid heat. He offered to sell her to Cassells, and found that his new friend was pleased to accept.

While I am sure Maurice Wilson knew he was making the right decision, it must have been a wrench for him to leave *Ever Wrest*. Those with enough affection for their machines to give them a name usually also invest them with some character and fellow feeling. The little Gypsy Moth had carried him safely over 5,000 precarious miles (8,047km); she had been pushed to the limit in extreme temperatures and with variable fuel, but through all the cramped, lonely and wearying hours of concentrating, and listening for any change in the steady sound of her engine, *Ever Wrest* had kept going.

With Cassells' good wishes ringing in his ears Maurice Wilson travelled by rail overland to Darjeeling, which was the starting point for all the 1920s and 1930s Everest expeditions. The journey took him through open countryside and sultry heat to the foothills of the Himalayas.

Lulled by the hum of a ceiling fan and the comfortable, regular sound of wheels against the track, he spent the first part of the trip looking out on wide, wet fields where white egrets stood by streams, insects droned and water buffalo chewed quietly under leafy awnings. This flat land was only varied by ponds, fences and villages built of woven fibre and bamboo. There were roads, bullock carts and bicycles, women in colourful saris bent over brilliant green rice shoots, and men working hard digging and repairing the channels that brought water from rivers and streams to their farms. In towns buildings jumbled together with balconies, towers, columns and domes, and, whatever their creed or caste, people hurried about their business – only the very old and the very young had much time to sit in the shade and watch the constantly changing drama of life around them. When the train stopped there was a great press of humanity; of jostling feet jumping down or climbing on board; of outstretched arms, fingers reaching for luggage, the support of a companion or pleading for money; of hundreds of lilting voices calling over each other, competing with the almost deafening noise of the steam engine, in the many languages of India, haggling over ticket prices, seats and the spicy snacks that sizzled on braziers at the back of platforms.

The second leg of Maurice Wilson's journey took him north from Siliguri, on the narrow gauge extension of the Northern Bengal State Railway that linked Darjeeling with Calcutta (originally the capital of British India). It had been built to carry tea for the East India Company and, later, the people who flocked to enjoy cool temperatures and a slow, elegant life as Darjeeling developed into a thriving hill station on India's northern frontier.

The small blue tank engines still pull their trucks and carriages twice a day up the atmospheric nine hour journey, rising roughly 6,500ft (2,000m) at a snail's pace that gives the traveller time to adjust to the change in scenery, temperature and culture. Through smoke smuts and heavy grey steam Maurice Wilson gazed out of the open window, and watched as the train climbed steeply up from the plain into shady forest, patchy at first with brick and wood built farmhouses and villages, and terraced fields leading to tended banana plants and then stretches of dark green trees, creepers and luxuriant undergrowth. Small gardens around the houses were colourful with lines of marigolds, geraniums in terracotta pots and scarlet flowering hedges. Everywhere children ran out to greet the train, shouting and waving while their parents and grandparents glanced up from their tasks.

The Himalayan foothills are steep and the railway was

built with a series of tight switchbacks, in places even crossing over itself to accommodate the gradient. As the train
climbed higher there were fewer farms, and the trees grew
more densely together, their branches crowded as they com-
peted for sunlight. Stations were simple country halts, a
length of wood and stones between the trees; and most had a
few people either waiting to meet someone or wanting to
board themselves, with bundles wrapped in colourful cloth,
or baskets of vegetables or chickens.

The air was cool and fresh, a welcome relief from the
humid heat of the plains, and it smelt of vegetation and damp
earth. Birds and monkeys shouted and chattered among high
leaves and twigs, hanging creepers brushed against the moving carriages, and exotic flowers and ferns grew in thick
undergrowth. Dodging branches as they passed, Maurice
Wilson leaned out where he could, craning to catch a view
upwards and ahead, but it was impossible to see through the
trees to either the top of the slope or the distant high mountains. As the hours passed, it became colder and darker, and,
with sunset, the forest grew both mysterious and forbidding.

Finally the train pulled into Darjeeling, where there was a
reassuring glow of lanterns hung along the platform and the
hot food and comfort of a station hotel. Without giving him
chance to either object or haggle, a small ragged boy pushed
through the milling crowd of passengers and porters, hoisted
Maurice Wilson's bag onto his shoulder with an air of experience and long practice, and led the way down the length of
the train and out into the town.

Darjeeling straggles along a ridge. I visited it in 1993, and
found that its steep narrow streets have a diverse mix of influ-
ences, from the faded elegance of the colonial hill station, the
simple but colourful ways of the Tibetan and Sherpa mountain

people and the rich, heady spice of India. Graceful buildings, in a way reminiscent of Harrogate, stretch out past wide verandas into well-tended gardens with tea plantations beyond, and window boxes are bright with flowers. In the crowded bazaar there is everything for sale – chickens, leafy vegetables, cloth, lumpy fists of ginger, plump white bulbs of garlic and brown unpeeled cardamom, alongside sacks of rice and lentils – and on street corners there are beggars, men playing dice and skinny cats lying in the sun.

There are open shrines with offerings carefully laid out and incense burning, for here the many deities of both Hindu and Buddhist faiths coexist peacefully in a haze of candlelight and sandalwood. You can see beautiful white topped peaks, dominated by the great bulk of Kangchenjunga, the 'Five Treasures of the Great Snows', which stands at the intersecting borders of Sikkim, Nepal and Tibet; and these days both Tenzing Norgay's statue and the Himalayan Mountain Institute's local centre stand as proof of Darjeeling's strong links with climbing.

Although the town was smaller, there was no concrete, the colonial buildings were newer and brighter and the stalls in the bazaar did not sell jeans, trainers or plastic toys, Darjeeling in 1933 was not so different, humming with visitors, especially in the summer months when the heat on the plains is at its most intense. It had grown quickly from a small sanatorium, established for British soldiers by the East India Company on land leased from the Maharaja of Sikkim, and was a thriving settlement. There the beliefs, traditions and way of life of local people from the nearby hill villages and farms blended both with those of families who had come up from the lowlands, and those which the Bhotias had brought with them from the hard mountain regions of Sikkim, Bhutan and Tibet.

Maurice Wilson loved it. Settling into some rooms in Albert Hall, a small establishment run by Mr W C Patton, he

Darjeeling Station.

happily accepted Darjeeling as his temporary home. As well
as the seasonal residents, there was a permanent British community in and around the town, with a succession of balls,
dinner parties, polo matches and afternoon teas. Frugal, and
perhaps a little wary of strangers, Maurice Wilson did not
participate much in the social round, sticking to his simple
and sober habits, but there was always something going on.
He was a fairly regular visitor at the Planters' Club, which
had served as a recruitment centre for the first British teams
wanting to employ Sherpas for climbing expeditions, and
every now and then he bumped into others seeking adventure
in the high mountains. Slowly he gleaned information, listening to what others had to say and bought, begged and bor-

rowed maps whenever he could.

To begin with Maurice Wilson hoped to get official permission to walk from Darjeeling, though the independent protected state of Sikkim and into Tibet. Patiently he petitioned the authorities, both in India and in London, enlisting the support of anyone who he thought could add weight to his pleas. Each time he was turned down. Some friends and acquaintances tried to dissuade him from the climb, pointing out all the experienced and well-supported climbers who had failed in their attempts on Everest. But Maurice Wilson was both stubborn and resolute, and each rebuff only strengthened his resolve. 'Stop me? They haven't a dog's chance.' He remained convinced that a small team, carrying only a minimum amount of luggage and buying basic food from villages and farms, had just as much chance of reaching the summit as a large, unwieldy expedition of climbers, Sherpas, ponies and yaks, weighed down by supplies, tinned European food and other equipment.

Writing to A J Russell, an acquaintance in London who he hoped would have some influence with the India Office, he said, 'In view of these hold-ups doesn't it seem to you somewhat uncanny that I am as optimistic as ever about my job of climbing Everest; the one I've been given to do?'[7] If he could not get permission he would go in secret. He knew that however he did it, he had to get to the mountain that had dominated his thoughts and dreams for so long. It was his destiny.

For the most part Maurice Wilson's weeks and months in Darjeeling passed pleasantly. He enjoyed pottering through the streets and the bazaar appreciating the heady, colourful mixture of life. There were morning visitors to the Hindu temple, family groups carrying baskets of marigolds and rice, ringing a bell on their way in and leaving later, cleansed and with renewed devotion, their foreheads marked with a fresh red powder tilak. As the day progressed, porters with baskets of vegetables and bananas dodged passing mule trains. These were led by dark eyed, long haired Tibetans shouting to clear the way, the animals loaded with bundles of salt and wool, their harnesses decorated with tassels and bells and their woven saddle blankets worked in colourful designs. Standing beside their stalls, traders haggled over prices.

There were Buddhist monks in long maroon and saffron robes, strings of smooth prayer beads hanging between their always moving fingers, and one or two stray cows ambled past, browsing over discarded vegetable tops. Men sat in doorways working at treadle sewing machines, a few chickens were held tethered by their legs to a stick driven into the ground, and children ran to and fro.

Some days Maurice Wilson simply sat in a basket chair on the terrace at the Planters' Club gazing out at the view beyond fields of low growing dark green tea bushes. He could either look down the forested hillside to the distant shimmering plains that ran all the way south to Calcutta and the Bay of Bengal, or he could choose to watch the other way, past lines of Buddhist prayer flags, to the high snow topped mountains. Alone in his rooms, he poured over maps, measured distances and made careful notes.

Although Maurice Wilson found the information he had useful, it was limited. In 1933, there were few detailed maps of the Himalayas, which in Western eyes were still relatively unexplored. Realistically, for him to travel overland to Rongbuk, which was near the base of the mountain, he would need a guide.

Members of the first British Everest expeditions quickly realised, and valued, the huge contribution of their Sherpa teams, recognising that their skills, strength and climbing experience went far beyond the portering and camping tasks that had originally been intended. They coined the term 'Tigers of the Snows' to honour those individuals who carried loads up to, and worked at, the highest altitudes.

In 1928, the British set up the Himalayan Club, with branches in Bombay, Calcutta and Darjeeling. Although its aim was to promote knowledge about the Himalayas, including the Karakoram and Hindu Kush regions, at the time the club's main role was to help climbing expeditions by publishing maps and descriptions of routes, and to formalise the recruiting of Sherpas as porters and guides.

Before this the Everest teams had chosen their Sherpas and porters in what sounds to have been a chaotic but entertaining public event. Some of the expedition members stood watching from the terrace of the Planters' Club while the rest walked slowly through a crowd of prospective applicants milling about in the street below. The hopeful recruits all pushed forward, jostling each other, shouting for attention and waving scrappy letters and written references from previous expeditions or employers, while those who had just come along to enjoy the spectacle squatted on the sidelines chewing paan and passing comments.

The Himalayan Club brought in written records of individuals' different experience, with each Sherpa having his own book to be signed before and after each expedition, and the local Club secretary oversaw the choice of teams, and negotiated wages with the relevant expedition leader to try and ensure some fairness.

Having decided he would have to travel in secret, Maurice Wilson knew he could not risk involving the Himalayan Club's secretary, as word of his plan was bound to leak out. However, one day he had a lucky introduction to Karma Paul, a Tibetan who had taken part in the 1922, 1924 and 1933 expeditions. Karma Paul was an invaluable and helpful source of information about the route to Rongbuk and beyond. For a while the two men planned to undertake the journey together, although it seems a disagreement brought their loose partnership to an end. Karma Paul was more

aware than most of the dangers involved in attempting
Everest, and he may have questioned whether Maurice
Wilson had sufficient technical mountaineering experience.
In turn it seems likely that Maurice Wilson would have react-
ed badly to anyone challenging his plans.

Meanwhile Maurice Wilson spent long days tramping by the
fields and plantations that reach along the hillsides around
Darjeeling, and out into the forest beyond, anxious to keep as
fit as he could. The ridge is a beautiful place from which to
look at the mountains. It is worth forcing yourself out from
warm sheets and blankets and climbing up to Tiger Hill to
watch the sunrise. From there the magnificent panorama of
high Himalayan peaks, stretching between earth and sky,
leads the eye from east to west, from Chomolhari in Bhutan
round to the north-west where the massive bulk of Makalu
stands at 27,765ft (8,463m), with Lhotse and Nuptse behind;
and some days, when the sky is clear, beyond them you can
see the dark, distant but distinct pyramid of Everest.

Despite his requests for permission to travel to Tibet being
refused, Maurice Wilson was allowed to join a small party on
a short trek in the Sikkim foothills. While he was away the
police both inspected his lodgings and kept a watch on the
trekking group to make sure he stayed with them. But at least
it gave him a slightly closer view of Everest. Anyone who
has tried peering at the mountain past other peoples' heads
pressed against an oval aeroplane window will empathise
with his low-key diary entry. 'Had my first glimpse of
Everest, but alas there was too much of a crowd to register a
true impression.'[8] Seeing Everest, really seeing it, not once
removed through a camera lens or window, takes time, and
some people prefer to be alone. But several days later,
Maurice Wilson did have his more moving 'true impression'.

A little before dawn, having slept alone outside, he woke to see the mountain through a gap in the first light mist. And then, as he watched, the clouds parted in the strengthening sunshine and he could see a semi circle of peaks, snow topped and golden, with Everest rising just above them all.

Back in his Albert Hall rooms he built up his strength and stamina as much as he could, with his long walks and a strict diet, alternating porridge, water and green vegetables with periods of fasting. At the turn of the year he decided he would set off in March, planning to leave the town in disguise and to travel by night, at least until he reached Tibet. To avoid suspicion he intended to pay six months' rent in advance for his rooms, leave behind those of his belongings that he would not need and tell his acquaintances in the town that he had been invited to join a tiger shoot.

1934 began badly for many people in the Himalayas, as a devastating earthquake rocked north-east India and Nepal. There were terrible landslides, rivers were blocked and wide areas that had been damaged by the earthquake then became flooded. In Darjeeling many of the buildings were destroyed and hundreds died. All the diverse people of the town pulled together, doing what they could, and the humanitarian Maurice Wilson was with them, his tall frame working tire-lessly over many days, relying on his good arm as much as he could, to shift wood, rubble and corrugated iron and to gen-tly carry the injured to those who could help them.

It was around this time that he met three Sherpas whose lives were to be inextricably bound with his; Tsering, Rinzing and Tewang. They had all taken part in the Ruttledge expedi-tion the year before and were keen to stay together, so Maurice Wilson decided to employ them all. It is possible that the introduction came through Karma Paul as in a report from the Deputy Commissioner of Darjeeling the following year, Tewang's occupation was given as 'servant of Karma Paul', while the other two men were each described as 'rickshaw wallas of the Gymkhana Club',[9] with Tsering also having had a military background.

In a statement Tewang gave later, he said that he had accompanied 'this Sahib' to Phalut[10] four months before (presumably when Wilson was trekking), and that this was how they had met. Either way, from the words of praise he regularly wrote about the three men in his diary, Maurice Wilson never regretted his decision. He and Tsering discussed the route to Rongbuk, while Rinzing and Tewang were asked to buy a sturdy pony that could carry their luggage.

Maurice Wilson's preparations were complete. It was time to continue his journey.

GOODBYE TO BRITISH INDIA

*To start on a long journey, in this part of Asia, is
always a step into the unknown.*
                                            Alexandra David-Neel

The diary that was found with Maurice Wilson's body begins
when he finally left Darjeeling. Having given up hope of any
official sanction, and taken matters into his own hands, his
quest was under way again at last.

As the crow flies it is roughly 120 miles (193km) from
Darjeeling to Rongbuk, but at the time it was not possible to
take such a direct route. Instead the expedition teams had to
go north and then west to avoid forbidden Nepal. Some
added further detours to explore unknown areas and peaks,
for measuring, recording and mapping were as much of a task
of, and justification for, those early expeditions as the Everest
climb itself.

Maurice Wilson decided not to take the usual expedition
route along the main mule and yak highway up the Chumbi
valley from Gangtok, an important trading town in Sikkim.
Instead he planned to follow a difficult but quieter and more
direct path beside the Tista river, north through the Lachen
valley and over the Kongra La pass into Tibet, picking up the
route of previous expeditions at Kampa Dzong. That way it
is a little over 300 miles (483km) to Rongbuk. The track is
spectacular, passing close to some of the high Himalayan
mountains, crossing the lower slopes of Chomiomo
(22,430ft;6,837m), with the great bulk of Kangchenjunga
(28,146ft;8,579m) to the south-west and Pauhunri

(23,180ft;7,065m) and Kangchenjau (22,700ft;6,918m) to the east. Although he realised parts of the route were likely to be strenuous and steep, Maurice Wilson hoped that a small group, without large numbers of pack ponies and mules burdened by luggage and equipment, would manage it.

He spent his last evening in Darjeeling squeezing everything he thought he would want or need for the next few months into his two kitbags, while trying to leave the rest of his belongings neat and tidy enough to support the tiger shoot tale. 'What a fuss I had packing up.' Maurice Wilson wrote his first diary entry at eleven o'clock, recording that one of his friends had come to help him disguise them, 'sewed up my two kitbags to look like sacks of wheat'. Traditonally, Tibetan herders and traders carried their staple supplies of tsampa (barley flour) strapped to the backs of their animals in drawstring leather sacks, covered with woven cloth. By letting air reach the tsampa, the leather bags kept it fresh, while protecting it from damp, and were strong enough not to split or tear with the rigours of travelling.

Maurice Wilson dressed in something like the robes of a Tibetan Buddhist monk, hoping to pass as a travelling lama. He thought this would both explain him having three 'attendants', and avoid unwelcome attention – for the many holy men journeying on foot in India and the Himalayas had free passage across borders, and tended to be less at risk from the bandits and warring clans who were renowned for robbing and killing unwary travellers in Tibet.

Shortly after midnight on Wednesday, 21 March 1934, Maurice Wilson tiptoed down the stairs of Albert Hall, wishing he had asked for ground floor rooms as he tried not to bump his luggage against the wall, and to keep his footsteps quiet, each creaking step seeming to echo far louder in the darkness than by day.

'What awful back stairs,' he wrote later. Once he had let himself out, with the latch clicked shut behind him, he sheltered from sight in the doorway, and waited ten minutes for Tsering to join him. Finally he spotted the Sherpa at the end of the narrow street, and shouldered one of the kitbags. With a nod and a smile Tsering picked up the other as easily as if it had been stuffed with feathers, tying his own smaller bundle of belongings to it.

It is easy to imagine the scene. Without speaking, the two men walked along the dark and mostly deserted Darjeeling streets, Maurice Wilson 'with bended knees to camouflage height'. The moon lit their way well enough as they passed through the sleeping town; on corners thin pye-dogs curled up together for warmth, their daytime rivalry forgotten; a solitary cat was on the prowl, moving with silent, graceful purpose, knowing how rats and mice raid the offerings left at wayside shrines; and the homeless, who had pulled their rags around them for the night, used whatever they could find in place of a pillow and shelter. Here and there candles or lanterns shone in windows, and where the air was not tinged with incense, it smelt of wood smoke, pack ponies and the rich spices of evening meals. Once or twice they started as a dog barked or someone shouted, and both men were relieved to pass the last of the town's sprawling settlements and have open country ahead.

Away from buildings they could see a vast expanse of wide, clear sky, peppered by thousands of stars; the moon was brighter now, showing the road clearly, with silhouettes of the mountains stretching into the distance. Shortly afterwards they had a sudden scare, spotting a policeman coming towards them. By the time they saw him they had no choice but to face him out – Maurice Wilson bent his knees again, and, with his head bowed, put his umbrella up while Tsering exchanged a greeting with the officer. 'Passed police over road and hid behind umbrella.' The forested foothills are so often shrouded in rain and damp clinging cloud that a traveller with an umbrella is not an unusual sight, even after dark.

Fortunately the policeman showed no interest and simply walked by.

The two men took the main road from Darjeeling down towards the bottom of the Tista valley, from where it continues up again to the Sikkimese centres of Kalimpong and Gangtok. The night time noises of the town had quickly been replaced by those of the country – an owl hooted, animals rustled underneath trees, there was the sudden movement of a bat out hunting, and always the lively tropical chirping of cicadas. The road, well used then by colourful mule trains carrying salt from Tibet, was a series of tight switchbacks past terraced tea plantations, wide stretches of damp, luxuriant forest, and small fields of rice and lentils hugging the steep hillside. It was easy going underfoot, and with nothing more than shadows on either side to distract them, Maurice Wilson and Tsering were able to stride out, wanting to cover the distance as quickly as they could and meet up with the rest of their party.

Then, as now, the mountain farmers' daily routine began a little after dawn. The women of the homesteads they passed were usually out first, pausing to make prayers and offerings of flowers, or a few grains of rice, at the household shrines before rousing their families and going out to collect water. Bright eyed children went in search of firewood, or eggs from rough basket chicken coops, while grandmothers spread grain and red chillis out on sacks and lengths of cloth to dry in the sunshine. Unwillingly dogs stood up, stretched and yawned, and the early morning foot traffic of people on their way to the fields and tea plantations started. In places, birdsong gave way to human voices. Wanting to avoid attention, Maurice Wilson and Tsering left the main road and walked on a rougher but more hidden path, parallel to it, and shielded by trees, ferns, hanging creepers and tall patches of gracefully arching bamboo.

They reached the group's agreed meeting point, roughly

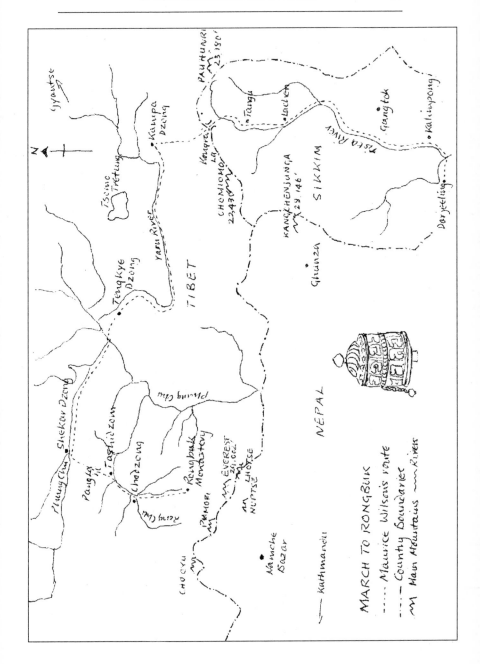

MARCH TO RONGBUK

—— Maurice Wilson's route
—·—· County Boundaries
ᴧᴧᴧ Main Mountains ～～ Rivers

nineteen miles (30km) from Darjeeling, at around eleven
o'clock in the morning, but there was no sign of the others.
Tsering led the search and after a little while he spotted
Rinzing, Tewang and the pony. 'All three asleep.' As he had
been anticipating an excited reception and enthusiasm for the
start of their venture, Maurice Wilson's first reaction was to
feel 'let down', especially as he suspected the two men had
been sleeping off the effects of the night before; but he
cheered up readily enough when Tsering fetched a couple of
cushions, and Rinzing prepared him some bread and a drink
– his first meal for 24 hours.

The plan was for the party to travel as much as possible under
cover of night, and so the four men spent their first day resting in the cool shade of the forest, alternately dozing, smoking, listening to the calls of birds and monkeys, and the
peaceful sound of distant waterfalls, and lazily watching the
dappled patterns of sunlight on the green and brown undergrowth, and the insects flying between exotic blooms. Now
and again they could hear shouts and laughter from the road,
children's high voices or the jingle of bells from a mule train.
    They set off again at seven o'clock, in the relative cool of
evening, with their luggage strapped firmly to the pony's
back. When the sun began to drop behind the mountains,
most of the local people headed back to their homes, and as
the little group walked past the first tiny scattered villages
that straddled the road they could see the evening activities
well under way – women cooking, clattering pans; neighbours talking over fences, their hands and faces as expressive
as their words; and children taking leafy forest bedding and
food to the family cow, or catching chickens to put them
away for the night. On the hills around Darjeeling, the houses were built of slatted wood and dried mud, and had roofs

thatched with sticks. Most were surrounded by thick hedges, and earthenware pots of scarlet, deep pink and orange flowers stood by doorways and under windows. A stream followed the road, diverted here and there into farmyard tanks through split bamboo pipes. Near these homesteads, wood smoke and savoury cooking scents mixed with the smells of vegetation and animals.

As it got later, and the darkness deepened, doors and shutters were closed, hiding the warm glow of fires and candle-light. But village dogs, sensing strangers and warning their fellows further on, barked long after they had passed by. The little group was able to stride out again on the switchback road and made good progress until about eleven o'clock when, as Maurice Wilson recorded, they 'nearly ran face to face with police. I fell flat in bed of nettles at roadside and well stung'. Fortunately the 'police hadn't heard' and they walked past without noticing a figure, dressed as a monk and pressed face down in a ditch. A few minutes later he was upright again, but no doubt with body and dignity stung. Brushing himself down, and grateful that they would soon be off the main highway, he resolved to keep out of sight as much as he could.

Later that day, Thursday, 22 March, having bypassed Kalimpong, Tsering took the pony to a village in search of supplies, leaving his employer sat amongst the trees. But travellers, even those dressed as holy men, are always a source of curiosity, and Maurice Wilson soon found that 'people came along and looked'. He pretended to be asleep as a little group of dark haired, wide eyed children squatted down in the undergrowth, and women stood behind them, putting down their bundles of ferns and leafy branches and covering their hair and lower faces with fine scarves, all waiting patiently to see what this interesting looking person would do. Finally he was rescued – 'Tsering came at last and told them I was deaf and dumb.' Maurice Wilson decided it would be best to stay inside altogether – 'Was safer alive all day with sand flies confined to tent.' But in the sticky heat, and plagued by biting insects, it must have been almost unbearable to spend the hottest parts of the day in a stuffy canvas cocoon.

The first part of their trek was a steep and relentless drop down roughly 7,000ft (2,134m) to the Tista river. Then, for the following five nights or so, they had a tiring, thirsty march through muggy forest. Sometimes the path rose over small passes, where the jungle and bamboo gave way to oaks and fir trees. There they had the relief of a few minutes of cooler breeze, with shadowy views across to snow topped Kangchenjunga if the sky was clear and the moon bright enough, before dropping back down again to subtropical trees, where the stagnant air is so thick with the smell of rotting leaves, wild cardamom and damp soil that I imagine they felt they could almost taste it.

The precipitous sides of the tributary valleys that lead down to the Tista are heavily forested, with mist shrouding their upper slopes. Tall, spindly trees stretch upwards, battling for light, and their boughs interlock, making a tunnel of greenery that hides the sky, hemming in anyone passing through. Creepers hang from branches and a wild, ungoverned profusion of vegetation thrives on the forest floor, decorated by bright flowers, and even brighter butterflies. Water cascades over rocks, with droplets spraying either side over ferns and thick mosses. Sometimes the four men could hear the hum of insects above the noise of the torrents, a deep croaking of bull-frogs or chattering from monkeys high in the trees.

Negotiating the wider streams meant either balancing across a couple of split and slippery logs with the pony in tow, or else enticing it over one of the flimsy, swaying bridges made of ropes and wood. These were hung with colourful prayer flags that fluttered sickeningly high above roaring white rapids, reminding them to offer pleas for a safe crossing. There are places where it is easier to step out in a cloak of darkness, trusting to faith, than it is to see what is either around you or in the expanse below.

Once they were away from the tea plantations and villages scattered between Darjeeling and Kalimpong there were thankfully fewer people – just occasional tea-houses offering travellers food and accommodation, and farms and small settlements on the higher, more open slopes. Nevertheless, Maurice Wilson kept to his precaution of travelling by night, and the little group established a routine of resting during the day, breaking camp around seven o'clock in the evening and then walking until two or three o'clock in the morning, usually covering fifteen or sixteen miles (25km or so). Generally Tewang and Rinzing went ahead with the pony. Maurice Wilson and Tsering left a little later, either catching the others up during the march or meeting them once they had camped and had a fire going for tea. Rinzing did most of the cooking, Tewang led the way and did other camp chores, and Tsering acted as guide.

On Friday, 23 March, Maurice Wilson noted, '7pm struck camp and had terrific climb for three hours' before resting at an inn – the three Sherpas went in while he waited outside with the pony, listening to the comfortable chatter of human voices and music drifting through the shutters, and admiring the 'glorious moon'.

It must have been difficult finding their way along narrow forest tracks in the darkness, sliding on rocks and mud or tripping over tree roots. When either the forest canopy or cloud was too thick for them to see the moon, there would have been hundreds of pinpricks of light from tiny fireflies, but darkness does not deter the voracious Sikkimese leeches,

which drop from leaves and branches above, or else catch
onto anything brushing through the undergrowth, wriggling
their narrow bodies into clothing and through boot eyelets.
For Sunday, 25 March, Maurice Wilson's diary says, 'Struck
camp last night 7pm and did sixteen miles – all v. tired as
uncertain track difficult.' He described the path as 'like
winding spiral staircase' in parts, noting later in the same
entry both 'difficult having to stay inside all day' and
'Looking forward to getting over the border and in Tibet as
prefer brigands to staying inside all day.' 'Get no kick out of
dodging police, etc.' he added, 'all seems part of game.'

Despite the tough night time walking, and the discomfort
of his cooped up days, Maurice Wilson seemed to settle into
life on the move. On Saturday, 24 March, he wrote cheerfully, 'Had lovely eggs and milk from bazaar for breakfast.
Party marvellous and couldn't wish for better. Very happy.'

Other than some close encounters with local people, when
he either hid under the earflaps of his large Tibetan hat or was
explained away as 'a sick friend deaf and dumb', and waiting
for the Sherpas outside the few inns they passed, Maurice
Wilson mentioned only a few events from the first part of
their trek in his diary. On Sunday, 25 March, he wrote,
'passed bands of coolies sleeping on road' beside the still
glowing embers of their cooking fires. By 'coolies' he meant
porters, for he mentioned them having some heavy electrical
cable bound for Lhasa – in 1934, most trade to Tibet was
through India and then on foot over the high passes.

In the early hours of the morning the porters overtook the
little Everest party, carrying the cable between them and
singing. Less so in Tibet, following the Chinese government's building schemes, but even now in the mountains of
Sikkim, Nepal, and Bhutan, tarmac and concrete only go so
far, and beyond the end of roads everything has to be carried
by men and women porters, or by pack animals, in heavy,
cumbersome loads.

The following day Maurice Wilson observed, 'Quite interesting to estimate nearness of dawn by the many jungle sounds – the bird calls are so pretty and I use one when wanting anything inside tent. Thank heavens no tent today and I can see the sunshine. Sun just coming over hill and shining on book as I write. Mountain stream few yards away. Have never been out of sound of rushing water since leaving D.' 'Been a bit upset with water,' he confided, 'but better today. Jungle life is wonderfully attractive and the best I've known yet.' As examples of his more mundane entries, on Monday, 26 March, 'Just had wholewheat bread. That stuff will play no small part in success' and, as they were climbing higher, 'Another couple of days and shall be wearing woollies.'

After that the route took them steeply and steadily upwards, away from the thick, humid forest and into more open woodland, where patches of rhododendron grow between scattered trees, tall magnolias have waxy cream flowers and scrubby grass and wild flowers replace the damp tangled undergrowth. There were fewer butterflies and insects, and they missed the constant, comfortable sound of droning, buzzing and chirruping that, like the noise of running water, had been ever present since they started out; but, thankfully, there were no more leeches. Maurice Wilson wrote with some feeling on Tuesday, 27 March, 'Damned tired when pulled into camp last night. Both done in and damned glad to see white tent. Boys had six boiled eggs waiting for us.' Anyone who has trekked in Nepal or Sikkim will empathise with his following comment, 'Tsering has funny notion of half a mile as we must have walked fully five miles after saying half.'

As the little group was trying to avoid settlements, and his maps were both limited and incomplete, it is not surprising that Maurice Wilson's diary rarely includes place names.

However, in his entry for 27 March, he noted that Tsering had 'just had tea with 'Big Man' from Lachen who knows his father'. Lachen is roughly half way between Darjeeling and Kampa Dzong, so they were making good time for 'the seventh day out,' and Maurice Wilson seemed to be proving just how fit he was. From his diary entries, they had also begun to walk by day sometimes, and so he must have felt more confident that they were out of reach of the authorities at last. I imagine it was a welcome change to be able to see where they were putting their feet, and to absorb the views around them.

That day, Maurice Wilson sounds to have been in a philosophical frame of mind as he wrote, for the Sherpas had all accepted an invitation to a neighbouring bungalow while he rested behind some bushes, ready to pull the wide sleeve of his robe over his chin and nose if anyone passed by. 'They'll all come sozzled,' he predicted, continuing more acceptingly, 'still they're good lads and it's all in the game I suppose.' He had the time for an unusually descriptive diary entry – 'Weather getting appreciably cooler as we climb. Can see snow on hill top, another 36 hours & shall be into it.' 'There's a beautiful burnt red bird fluttering around – vivid vermilion.' 'Glorious spot, mountains almost vertical either side.' 'Beautiful cascade playing right ahead of me.' 'There is a thick heat haze in valley we are leaving. Shall be quite at home in the cold of plains in Tibet.'

From Lachen the path rises through a pleasant grassy area with Himalayan blue poppies, buttercups and wild strawberries, before steepening into a thirteen mile (21km) ascent from 8,000ft (2,438m) to 12,800ft (3,900m). As the four men climbed steadily upwards, panting and dizzy, it got colder and more exposed with only a few windswept trees managing to survive alongside the evergreen shrubs. There the rhododendrons and azaleas are low, twisted and windblown, but their leathery dark green leaves have a distinct perfume and are burned as offerings in the mountain temples and monasteries. Between the bushes are more blue poppies as well as wild roses and primulas, and, if the four men had paused to look further ahead, a panorama of crags and snow peaks stretched beyond them. Up in the hills, after the close, damp forest, the world has wide horizons.

'Camp very much exposed,' Maurice Wilson wrote later, recording that it had been a 'terrible climb up.' Most of his entry for Wednesday, 28 March, revolved around their camp. 'Had lovely bath with a washtub today and needed it. Done a bit of darning today. Pity mother never showed me how though I'm improving.' He also described Tsering showing him a 'funny looking gadget' – 'huge leather bag open at top with metal outlet at bottom like bellows. Says no wood in Tibet. Must use pony dung dried for cooking. Don't know whether they tie it under horse's tail like nose-bag or whether they stop the procession & pick it up – if so hope the cook doesn't get the job!'

The following morning Maurice Wilson was up at three o'clock, rousing the others and keen to set off. They had a long and exhausting ascent of about fifteen miles (24km). The altitude would have meant their progress was fairly slow, with frequent stops to catch their breath and ease their aching legs, and although he did not mention an altitude headache members of the 1935 expedition all reported this when they had got above 12,000 ft (3,658m). Maurice Wilson simply wrote, 'Pleasant trekking. So much cooler'. For the first time they walked through snow – 'shall be permanently in it tomorrow.'

It was Thursday, 29 March 1934, and at the end of the day's hike, as he crouched in his tent trying to avoid the curious gaze of another party camping nearby, Maurice Wilson

pulled back one of the canvas flaps and, in the last of the fading daylight, looked up at the rocky slope rising steadily from
their campsite to a snowy pass beyond. I imagine sitting
there, squinting upwards, he could convince himself there
were tell-tale red, blue, yellow, green and white prayer flags
fighting with the wind against the clear, frosty sky – it was the
Kongra La. Immediately beyond the pass, just down the
slope on the other side, he would be in Tibet.

The following morning they had a stiff climb up to the
pass, the altitude demanding more effort with each mile. I
imagine Maurice Wilson with his eyes fixed on the ground in
front of him, plodding upwards doggedly, concentrating on
moving one foot in front of the other along the rocky track,
with slow, deliberate breathing to try and ease his head and
help his struggling lungs. Each painful footfall was another
step towards his destination.

The effort of keeping going meant the little party had neither energy nor enthusiasm to talk or admire the scenery.
However, if they did pause briefly to look around them, gasp-
ing and struggling to stand still against the high wind, the
views would have been incredible.   The summit of
Chomiomo stood above them to the south-west, and beyond
it lines of mountains stretched as far as the eye could see,
their dark crags and wide snow slopes sharp and brilliant
against the bright blue sky. And ahead were dry and rocky,
but more rolling, hills leading in undulating waves across to
the arid, sand coloured Tibetan plain.

The top of the Kongra La pass was marked by lengths of
prayer flags tied to boulders and low posts. These are either
strips or squares of thin cloth in the bright colours of the five
elements, with prayers printed on one side, commonly around
the picture of a lungta (a windhorse) carrying wish-fulfilling
jewels. They are found throughout the Buddhist Himalayas,
tugging against the breeze on hillsides, bridges, mountain
passes and rooftops. With every flap each lungta gallops off

into the wind, and then around the world, with blessings and wishes for the benefit of all beings.

Maurice Wilson did not record it, but perhaps the three Sherpas added their own pebbles to one of the small rock cairns (obos) that are generally also found on passes in Tibet, sometimes with prayers worked on them, conciliatory offerings to the spirits that live there, and a request for safe passage. Maybe Maurice Wilson acknowledged them too, for so far, his own prayers had been answered.

INTO TIBET

Tibet is a land of dreams, for in its golden vistas, in its silences, in its white walled monasteries, is the stuff of dreams.

Frank Smythe

Slithering on loose stones and shingle, and exhausted but elated, Maurice Wilson began the steep climb downhill, one set of leg muscles exchanging the pain of effort with another. Behind him was Sikkim, and India beyond it, with thick forests butting up to terraced fields of rice, lentils and vegetables, where, both on the plains and in the foothills, the family year revolved in a familiar, dependable cycle of planting, tending and harvesting. Where there were abundant leaves in every shade of green with bright, extravagant flowers between, and the hazy air droned with insects, and smelt of warm earth, growing plants and spice.

Ahead was unknown Tibet, with its cloudless, gentian sky, and an atmosphere so dry that its vast distances seemed to take no space at all. He could see no trees, no fields and almost no grass, just a few dusty plants eking out an existence between boulders, clinging low to the ground against the punishing wind. Everything looked barren – mile after mile of rocky hills, honey coloured in the harsh sunshine. Tibet was a land of nomads, families moving their yaks, horses and sheep between summer and winter pastures, and barley was the only crop tough enough to thrive in the thin soil.

Maurice Wilson was overjoyed to have crossed the border, his diary entry having an almost childlike triumphant tone.

'Now in forbidden Tibet and feel like sending government a wire, 'Told you so' or 'How'd you like your eggs boiled?'

Exhilaration kept them all going as they slid and staggered down the stony mountainside towards Gompa Lawu. Gradually the four men began to feel better as they got lower, despite the strong dusty wind that stung their faces and parched their throats.

They camped at 15,000ft (4,572m), which, as Maurice Wilson noted, was 8,600ft (2,621m) higher than the altitude they were used to in Darjeeling. Despite the heavy frost, he spotted some Tibetans curled up asleep on the ground beside the track, one or two with blankets round them but the rest just in their daytime clothes, their belts loosened and arms tucked into ample sleeves. Although he planned to stick with his monk's robes, he spent time in his tent organising his kit bags and pulling out warm clothing in case it was needed before they got to Rongbuk.

'Had a mug of tea when we camped,' he wrote cheerfully, having reported that the 'gadget' he had described in his previous diary entry was a 'pair of primitive bellows.' The tea 'took a hell of a time to make. Fuel not much good & I suppose altitude has something to do with it.' The following morning he woke to find that the clothes he had taken off were starchy stiff with cold, and that the few plants growing near their tents were edged with frost.

After the excitement of crossing the border, I imagine it was difficult to accept that they were not yet half way to Rongbuk. There were many long and arduous miles ahead. Maurice Wilson tackled the task with characteristic impatience, changing his priority from secrecy to speed. He wanted to get the job done. On Saturday, 31 March, he wrote, 'Have done about 25/30 miles at least today over plateau 15/18,000ft up. For the last four or five hours we have been in sight of camping ground, & at the start could have sworn not more than a mile – all afternoon and only seemed like keeping up to the damned place.' He added confidently 'Time flying. Shall be at E 10/12 days.'

The following day they rested at the campsite. In his diary Maurice Wilson said this was because the pony had sores, although they must all have been exhausted. He blamed his own restless, broken sleep on going to bed too early, just after he had eaten, and on the fierce wind and dust that buffeted the camp, but I suspect the altitude contributed to his insomnia.

In contrast to the earlier part of their trek, while they travelled through Tibet, Rinzing and Tewang usually set up camp on the outskirts of villages or hamlets, hoping this would give them some safety from attack by either bandits or wolves, both of which were common. Many Tibetans feared strangers, believing that demons attached themselves to travellers, and in some places people hid in their homes, barring shut windows and doors, as their dogs barked ferociously.

On Sunday, 1 April, having been with Tewang to buy food, Rinzing spent the day cooking goat's meat ready for the next few days' march. Sitting outside his tent with Tsering enjoying some fresh air and watching Rinzing at work over the fire, Maurice Wilson was unceremoniously pushed back under the canvas as two villagers approached; meanwhile Tsering chanted prayers loudly, hoping their uninvited and curious guests would leave. 'Glad when we are on move again,' Maurice Wilson wrote later.

The little party set off the following day, Monday, 2 April, starting at dawn and walking for two and a half hours before stopping to light a fire and have some breakfast.

Maurice Wilson mentioned passing some 'quaint villages'. Tibetan homesteads are traditionally built of whitewashed pounded clay, with flat roofs and, where there is space, a high, solid wall around an open courtyard, secured by a heavy, iron studded wooden door. The door and window frames are often carved and painted, decorated with bright flowers and geometric designs in primary colours, and wide strips of white, red and blue cloth, fastened horizontally above the tops of windows, flutter in the breeze. There are generally prayer flags or bunches of long dried grasses fixed high at each roof corner, as well as along the wall tops. Most have neat stacks of dried yak dung outside, ready to burn, and in the mornings and the evenings curling wisps of grey smoke rise from cooking fires. In some villages, homes are tucked in tight, with walled squares replaced by narrow, beaten earth yards where there is just enough room to tether a cow or two, or to keep some chickens. 'All the houses jumbled together,' Maurice Wilson observed. 'No such things as neighbours' rights to worry about.'

In 1934, each home in villages, more isolated farmsteads and nomad camps, would have had at least one large black Tibetan mastiff, with strong jaws and fearsome white teeth. Their owners put scarlet yak hair ruffs around their necks, making them seem even bigger. Traditionally these dogs were prized for their ferocity, and, as a mark of breeding, the depth of their bark, which should ideally resonate like a great temple gong.

Mani walls stood on the way in to most villages, and sometimes at cross roads, or between obos on high passes. These low walls are lovingly built of stones carved or painted with the mani invocation of Chenrezig, the bodhisattva of compassion. 'Om mani padme hum' represents the essence of the buddhas' compassion for all beings. Chenrezig is the most important and beloved bodhisattva of the Tibetan people and, in 1934, this mantra was carved, scratched and painted on walls, stone, wood and metal throughout the country. Like countless thousands of others, Tsering, Rinzing and Tewang would have chanted it daily. Mindfully they would also have made sure the little group always kept to the left of these walls, and of the chortens that stood from place to place beside the path, pausing sometimes to seek merit by pushing back stones that had slipped out of place, or by leaving a little tsampa as an offering.

On 2 April, Maurice Wilson described their day as 'another tramp over the desert.' In the bright, shimmering distance were light brown and purple coloured hills, and although much of the area they were crossing was flat, there was a river and great banks of sand beside the rough dirt road. 'Hot sun and cold wind. Lovely golden sand.' But whipped up by the wind, the bright grains would have choked them, blasting their already burned faces with a thousand red hot needles, and found a way into their hair, eyes and luggage. 'It's blowing like the devil & sand everywhere,' he wrote after they had camped that evening.

The pony took exception to something, and made a bolt for freedom. 'Maybe he doesn't like the dry straw after the succulent greenery of Sikkim so took it into its head to go back.' The four men gave chase, panting with the exertion at altitude, and caught up with it after about a mile.

They covered a good distance but camped quite early, once again near a village, where, having enjoyed the homebrew hospitality of a funeral party, Tsering bought supplies – 'eggs, meal, meat etc. Also chillis as they complain of pains at temples on account of altitude though haven't noticed it myself yet.' Maurice Wilson had a leisurely evening writing a longer than usual diary entry, enjoying an omelette, preparing his camera for the following day and watching the Sherpas as they busied themselves with camp chores. 'They are just having an evening meal. One of them cutting up the meat they cooked yesterday whilst another makes dough out of coarse flour and Tibetan tea, which he kneads in a goatskin bag.'

It seems from his diary that Maurice Wilson felt contented and at peace. 'The boys are already talking about what we're going to do on way back. Shall return by other route. It is lovely that everyone is optimistic. Not many men would have let the pony go without a beating after running away.'

The following day, Tuesday, 3 April, was another long march, with the two or three hours before they camped becoming a battle to keep moving against the wind, and to avoid tripping up in the hundreds of mousehare burrows that peppered stretches of the open plain. Perhaps not surprisingly, 'Pony tried turn tail again but I caught it in time.'

To keep up their ambitious speed the little party left at first light the next morning, taking advantage of the hours before the inevitable wind took hold, although Maurice Wilson paused to take a photograph of the village they had camped near, its white houses, surrounded by trees with some marshy green grass and bright yellow flowers, all touched with the pale peach and gold of dawn, and perfectly reflected in a small lake – 'Perched up on little hill with water below. Looked pretty in early morning light.'

On Wednesday, 4 April, their route brought them back into the mountains, stopping to make their breakfast at a mountain spring, glad of some cold water after the tough climb up. 'Scenery gorgeous.' From where they were there are wide, limitless horizons; the glittering northern wall of the Himalaya standing firm in the distance; arid foothills in front, with the heavy grey, warm brown and gold colours of their rocks blending together. The different, ancient strata of stone show clearly, and in places are warped and twisted, testament to conflict within the earth when the great mountains formed. On the ground saxifrages flower in soft clumps between pebbles, russet lichen decorates boulders and patches of thin grass give some relief to the eye. I imagine them standing together, taking it in, with a deep blue sky above, and the only shadow coming from a solitary lammergeier, the bearded vulture, drifting high on the thermals.

After the steep climb up it must have been a relief to have a slow and steady tramp down into a valley, although by then the breeze had strengthened again, buffeting them relentlessly until the sun began to sink. In the distance they perhaps caught sight of a small herd of gazelle, for the animals were still common in the area then. As usual, the little party camped that night near a village, Maurice Wilson noted in his diary later, 'Two shabby little Tibetan girls came and held tent in the wind for the boys. Such musical voices. Having boiled eggs and rice brought as too sandy for omelette.'

For the next three days the little party kept up a steady pace, tramping solidly for long and often dreary hours. Each morning they broke camp early, stopping to eat once they had done a couple of hours, and resting as they waited for the water to boil. They mostly walked together, feeling they were less at risk of attack that way, although they were always wary, and I picture them watching for wild, long haired horsemen appearing from behind boulders or over mountain passes. 'Must keep together now as we are in land of brigands.'

The countryside was fairly monotonous – rolling rocky hills and wide sandy plains, broken here and there, once they had passed Kampa Dzong, by the Yaru River. When they were high enough they had good views back to the Sikkimese mountains – Pauhunri, Kangchenjau and Chomiomo. There were fewer villages, and the bright clear air was deceptive, shrinking distances. 'Camped what looked to be within hailing distance of previous night,' Maurice Wilson wrote in frustration.

Every day they fought the wind, bracing their bodies against it and dragging the pony with them. There was usually a lull in the early mornings but later in the day it came screaming at them from the west, right into their faces, beating them with sand, and sometimes snow; giving them earache and sore throats, and drying their lips so much they split and cracked into painful sores that made sipping warm drinks agony. At night it shook their tents, moaning louder than the distant howls of wolves.

The days were hot, and there was little shade from the fierce, burning sun; with sunset it quickly became bitterly cold, but the sky was so clear that the stars seemed to be nearer and brighter than anywhere else in the world. Maurice Wilson reported 'Feeling exceptionally fit', and he preferred to be out walking during the day than hiding in his tent. But he also mentioned, 'Had bit of head last few days. Hat is a bit thin for the sun.' And, which seems hard to conceive given the advice to those staying at altitude now, 'Haven't had drink all day but just gone off rails with pot of tea.' When they had stopped for the day he rested, took photographs, wrote his brief diary entries and listened to the voices and laughter of the three Sherpas squatting by the fire, as appetising smells drifted out of their cooking pots.

Tengkye Dzong is essentially the mid-point between Darjeeling and Rongbuk. In Tibet in 1934, as now in Bhutan, a dzong is in part a fortress, a seat of local government and a religious centre. Each of Tibet's regions was governed by a dzongpen (local administrator), but as the Buddhist religion was an integral part of everything – including the country's government – important lamas were in many places as powerful, if not more so, than the secular administrators.

At Tengkye, the dzong stood at the entrance to a wide valley, overlooking a small lake. A large gompa (temple) stood on the hillside nearby and a higgledy-piggeldy hamlet sprawled between the two. Members of the official Everest expeditions described it as a beautiful place, sheltered from the wind, with trees and a few fields. I can picture Maurice

Wilson and his Sherpa companions, perhaps watching as a couple of local farmers used a team of yak and a wooden plough to turn over the soil, working in circles out from the centre of the plot and singing as they went. This pattern of ploughing was to drive any bad spirits to the edge of the field so they could not harm the barley crop. A small child sat in an open doorway as its grandmother worked at her loom. Chickens searched about for scraps, and an old man lent against a tree stump with his prayer beads, his brown parchment face wrinkling as his mouth moved silently; then, looking up briefly, he broke into a gentle, peaceful smile. Lizards basked on rocks, enjoying the sunshine, and around the trees there were larks singing, small finches fluttered between branches and a hoopoe strode through some grass. After their days in the 'desert' it must have seemed like heaven, and have been almost unbearably tempting to sit down and doze quietly until the evening.

For most of the way between Kampa Dzong and Shekar Dzong their route ran beside the broad Yaru river, and then, further west, the Phung river. 'Had to ford a river,' Maurice Wilson wrote on Sunday, 8 April. 'I rode pony whilst others stripped.' 'Tsering gone with boys for stores,' he added later. 'Suppose they will have a few sports on way as it is some days since had any. Everybody optimistic. Talking of what will do on way back.'

At this point he estimated they would be within sight of Everest in three days, and I imagine it was an exciting prospect. The countryside was rougher and, once again, there were fewer villages. 'Away in wilds,' he noted on Monday, 9 April. Like the Sherpas he daydreamed about the long march back, anticipating the accolades but perhaps a little homesick too. 'How time is going. Looking forward to a good wag. Cannot speak very much to boys. Just as well I'm used to my own company.'

Above, Darjeeling in the morning mist and, below, at the edge of the forest, Sikkim.

In the forest, Sikkim.

Above, a traditional Tibetan house and, below, prayer flags and a chorten on a pass, Sikkim.

Above, Everest from tourist base camp and, below, the Tibetan plain.

Feeling their goal was almost within reach, Maurice Wilson allowed them all a day of rest from the punishing pace, conscious that they still had to cross the 17,200ft (5,240m) Pang La. On Tuesday, 10 April he mentioned that it was sixteen years since he had gone 'into line' in France. But he kept any memories and reflections to himself; his other diary entries for that day spoke only of their supplies and the number of people who had visited the camp, here curious of travellers, and what they might carry with them, rather than fearful. He reported that they were camped 'near large village'. The little group were in Shekar District, and it is likely that they were camped near the settlement around Shekar Dzong itself.

At the time, Shekar was a large and important area, with the dzongpen's administration extending as far as the Rongbuk valley and Everest. While Maurice Wilson now travelled fairly openly, drawing attention to himself within sight of the Tibetan authorities was too big a risk, particularly as local officials were known for expecting anyone they thought might be wealthy to pay bribes for permission to pass through their territories. Although Tsering went to buy supplies, Maurice Wilson kept close by his tent, and they skirted the settlement when they did get under way again.

The scenery around Shekar is stunning – an expanse of barren, rocky plateau, which combines countless shades of brown, russet and gold, with so many textures of stone and sand, that it is beautiful, timeless and uplifting to look across it at the mountains and jagged ramparts that lie beyond. The dzong itself stands on a single pyramidal rock around 1,000ft (305m) above the plain with views all around; and would have given the authorities fair warning of attack in troubled times. The old Tibetan travellers saw the fortress of Skekar as a wonder of their world, and they carried incense to its highest battlements and look out points, burning it there and offering the fragrance to Miyolangsangma, the goddess they believed lived on Everest, as well as to the mountain itself.

'One can see her from here,' Reinhold Messner wrote, having climbed up to the ruined dzong in 1980. 'She stretches out her white arms on both sides, a goddess in the form of stone and ice.'[1]

In 1934, Shekar Dzong was as wild and mysterious as the scenery in which it stood. Around the base of the rock was a jumble of white washed houses, spreading in a haphazard maze out onto the plain, with smoke rising comfortably from holes in rooftops, men and women exchanging news in the narrow alleys between their homes, children playing and animals standing patiently, tethered by doorways. On the slopes above them stood two monasteries, and then beyond was the dzong itself. Steep, white walls rose from the rocky hillside towards a clear blue sky. High up were small windows, and above them towers and crisscrossed walls, with roofs, windows and doors at different heights as they narrowed together with the slope of the hillside. At the top of each of the white walls was a wide stripe of deep russet brown; white, royal blue and red cloth hung above the windows; and gold conical structures, figures of deities and dragons' heads set on the corners of roofs, glittered in the sun.

A solitary maroon and saffron clad figure stood gazing over the plain, a curl of juniper smoke drifted towards the sky, and the wind carried the haunting notes of long Tibetan horns punctuated by sharp clear bells calling the attention of the universe, and all the realms beyond, to the monks' timeless, chanted prayers. Still higher up the hillside were lines of coloured flags and white chortens, while walled battlements somehow clung to the rock as far as a lookout tower at the top; only the mountain birds commanded a higher view. After the 1933 expedition, Hugh Ruttledge described it as 'a setting for a fairy story, a place of enchantment.'[2]

Now the old settlement at Shekar has been replaced by orderly rows of uniform grey concrete buildings. There are just a few last ruined ramparts and stone walls high up on an abandoned crag above the village. They stand against the skyline like rows of ancient broken teeth, but are somehow at one with the rocks and the arid, treeless landscape; as though they are still united against invaders from beyond the mountains.

The little group set off again on Wednesday, 11 April, heading due south towards Everest, stopping early in the day to eat and rest. 'No b'fast tomorrow as have a climb to do,' Maurice Wilson wrote, adding, 'Had a bit of a head today, with sun I think.'

The following morning they broke camp early for the climb over the steep Pang La. They would have toiled their way slowly and steadily up the rough, switchback track, breathing as deeply as they could in the thin air, most probably their heads thumping and their chests tight and painful, with the shale underfoot so fine that in places I imagine it felt as slippery as snow. It is a tough climb, even for someone used to walking at altitude, and while the cloudless sky meant they could see for miles, there would have been neither respite nor relief from the blinding sun. At the top of the pass there are stunning views across the Himalayas if the weather is good, and a tangle of prayer flags flap together, their noise sharp above the wind.

The Sherpas told Maurice Wilson he was fortunate to be there in spring, for it is the best time of year for clear views. 'Saw E today from 17,800ft,' he wrote afterwards. 'Looked magnificent. One half in snow plume.' I was surprised, and a bit disappointed that he had added, 'Don't get the slightest kick out of the whole adventure and am already planning for future after the event. I must win.' At first I wondered if, having got so far, and at last being almost within touching distance of the mountain he had dreamed of for so long, he suddenly yearned for the familiar security and certainty of home, anxious to get back to his 'older friendships'. Or did he maybe feel a twinge of awe, or fear, or an unfamiliar, niggling doubt? But on other days he also wrote of not being touched by mountains, and of 'longing to get the job over,' so perhaps he was genuinely unmoved by the majesty of his surroundings.

That night, exhausted after their climb over the Pang La, the little group stopped near the surprisingly verdant oasis of Tashidzom where there are soft green willow trees, fields of barley and vegetables, and a small meadow for the pony to enjoy. It would have been the last lush vegetation they saw.

The following day, Friday, 13 April, they camped by the village of Chodzong, where sparse grass finally gives way completely to rock. There the village homes and animal folds are not built of traditional, white-washed clay or mud bricks but of rounded grey river stones, somehow balanced together in an impossible jigsaw to support rickety roofs and crooked doorways. It looks too barren a landscape to support life for there is no grazing to speak of, even for the hardy yaks. Ahead of the four men there was only boulder, scree, snow and ice. Maurice Wilson wrote a fairly long diary entry that evening, mentioning several colourful interruptions from the villagers, although his mind was focussed on what lay ahead the following day.

'Camped again, last time before Rongbuk. Shall have pukka place to sleep tomorrow night.' Perhaps realising now that his food and equipment might not be adequate he planned to 'borrow' from stocks he understood the well-supplied 1933 expedition had left. 'Shall tell the lama I am one of the expedition if anything wanted from stores and flour or choc or anything like that. Tsering says there is plenty of meat at Rongbuk. What a game. Maybe in less than five weeks the world will be on fire.'

From Chodzong it is only about fourteen miles (23km) to Rongbuk. The valley quickly gets narrower and steep sided, with rocky terraces climbing up from either bank of the milky glacial river. The little group plodded along steadily, trying not to trip on loose stones and helping the pony pick its way safely. For some hours they seemed to be heading towards a dead end of bleak rock walls, as the wind moaned around them, and chased clouds across the sky. Then, almost without warning, they walked round a final corner and saw Rongbuk monastery ahead of them, with Everest beyond it, an immense ice and rock pyramid, black and white against gentian blue. 'Everest looks magnificent,' Maurice Wilson wrote later.

It is a dramatic spot, and from that point, almost as though passing through a gateway, the valley ahead is wider, although still steep sided. The monastery complex is set up a little to one side; and in 1934 was a series of squat, square sided white buildings climbing onto low rock ledges beyond a big chorten, with prayer flags on the slopes above. The four men stood for a few minutes, watching in silence; monks moved across open courtyards, dogs dozed in the shade and pilgrims picked their way on a kora, a clockwise route around the chorten and the main gompa, some prostrating while others spun their hand prayer wheels and chanted as they walked.

Beyond the monastery, their eyes would have followed the river, one narrow path running parallel to it, while others led to a nunnery and the isolated hermits' caves and cells that dotted the rocky hillsides. And in the distance was Everest itself, defined by sheer pointed ridges, pure white ice and snow between black crags, its distinctive peak so much higher than any other mountain around it. To Maurice Wilson, this imposing, inspiring and surely frightening sight of the mountain he was destined to climb must have meant more than all his more distant views. At last, and against all the odds, he had reached the remote, mystical and sacred Rongbuk valley. Like a pilgrim he stood at Chomolongma's feet; Miyolangsangma, from her home on the summit, looked down at him.

With a slap of encouragement to the pony the little group got moving again, placing their feet carefully on the stony path until they reached the monastery compound and found a flat area suitable for their tents. Tsering went to see the monks, to explain Maurice Wilson's plan and to seek permission both to camp and to use the 1933 expedition's stores. Unfortunately he did not find any food, but the Sherpa came back with a couple of Tommy cookers and a tent.

'Here we are at Rongbuk,' Maurice Wilson wrote, as the sun set behind the mountains. 'Monastery is quite interesting sight.' Reporting that his lantern only gave a very small light with the altitude, Maurice Wilson, reflected happily, 'Boys all looking forward to me getting it over and back quickly. Chaps been wonderful throughout.'

THE FIRST ATTEMPT

*Everest assumed an extraordinary living character,
a living thing of fascinating beauty, of fearful
power.*   *John Noel*

It was an achievement for Maurice Wilson to have reached
Rongbuk. Away from the authorities in Darjeeling, he, and
his three Sherpa companions, had marched for over 300 miles
(483km) through mountainous Sikkim and Tibet, initially
travelling mostly by night and often avoiding settlements;
always wary of their identity being discovered. They had
done it in just 25 days, ten days less then Hugh Ruttledge's
expedition the year before. From the point of view of accli-
matising to the altitude, there are benefits in taking time, and
a bigger team, with more porters and animals, would have
been slower even if they had been able to follow the more
direct Tista river route, but this speed shows how fit Maurice
Wilson was, and how he seemed to thrive on the physical
challenge.

For the early Everest expeditions, it was always a race
against time after the end of the winter weather in Darjeeling,
to reach Rongbuk and try for the summit before the June
monsoon temperatures made the ice unstable and sent avalanches thundering down snow slopes. By travelling quickly
Maurice Wilson gave himself extra time on the mountain,
although from the confident (but frankly unrealistic) entries
in his diary he expected to be just six or seven days up and
back, and did not anticipate needing more than one attempt.
After a night camped near the monastery, he reported feeling

well, having spent several days on nothing but rice, barley meal, oats and bread, and had slept soundly in the Meade tent Tsering had 'borrowed' from the 1933 expedition's store, noting appreciatively that its integral groundsheet would stop the wind from blowing in any sand or snow.

Maurice Wilson was typically focussed, allowing himself only one day's break, enough time to organise his things, write a long entry in his notebook and prepare for the only reason he was there. His diary neither acknowledges nor celebrates the success of reaching the end of their march across the roof of the world. Instead, he only looked forward, opening his entry for Sunday, 15 April with the mountain that absorbed his thoughts and plans. 'Isn't she a darling? She's magnificent.' 'Have a marvellous view of her again today.'

From the distance of the Tibetan plateau, in the bright air the eyes play tricks, and it is difficult to appreciate the height of Everest. With other summits nearby, like Makalu, Cho Oyu, Lhotse, Karma Changri and Pumori, it seems to be just one amongst many massive mountains. George Mallory wrote, 'The whole range of peaks from Makalu to Everest far exceeds any mountain scenery that I ever saw before.'[1]

But from Rongbuk monastery, one mountain dominates everything. The valley is flat bottomed, about a mile (1.6km) wide and twenty miles (32km) long, with a milky, ice cold river running down it. There is very little vegetation, and at first glance everywhere is grey rock, moraine dumped by the mountains' glaciers many years ago, the only bright colour being from prayer flags moving in the breeze. Rongbuk valley is flanked by high steep slopes, and on a clear day the gaze is drawn straight ahead to Everest; a triangular mass of granite, ice and snow, a white plume of spindrift rising from the summit and fading into blue sky. I imagine on that day, the eve of beginning his climb, it was impossible for Maurice Wilson to think about anything else.

Rinzing left the little group early that morning, heading for a four-day trip to the market at Tingri 'to load in for the troops'. It sounds to have been a warm and affectionate parting. Maurice Wilson 'shook him by the hand and thanked him for his loyalty so far,' but no doubt Rinzing wondered if he would see his employer again. Meanwhile Maurice Wilson had 'a damned good bath and rub down,' and packed his rucksack, congratulating himself on having got so far, and so high, without resorting to either his jumpers or wool clothing. 'Came right through to Rongbuk in cotton poplin pants, and short open vest and undies. No pullover and am now feeling the benefit.' There was no longer a need for any local disguise, and he could dress openly in European clothes again. 'Anyone would think I was on a picnic wearing mauve flying shirt, green flannel pants and white tennis shoes.'

When Tsering had visited the monastery the previous afternoon, he came back with an invitation from the abbot, Dzatrul Rinpoche. 'Summoned to see the lama. We are all going.' Every expedition that had passed through the holy Rongbuk valley called at the monastery to pay their respects, and seek a blessing, and Tsering expected Maurice Wilson to do the same. Anything else would anger the spirits and the gods, inviting wrath against the foreign visitor, his Sherpa guides and the people living in the shadow of the mountain.

When the first expeditions reached this final approach to Everest in the 1920s, some of the porters had cowered in their tents, refusing to go any further, convinced they could hear blood curdling howls from the dogs that guard Miyolangsangma. A dozen years later, more were prepared to risk it, but there had been deaths on the mountain. Men had played a heavy price for the foreigners' temerity. It has always been wise to approach with reverence and respect, and to seek protection through prayers and offerings.

Looking back from a Western and secular 21st century, it is not that easy to appreciate what a holy place Rongbuk monastery and the area around it were at the time. The region was known as Chamlung, Sanctuary of the Birds. Each expedition was warned that there must be no taking of life, either in the valley or on the mountain slopes, for it was a place of peace. Even the roasting of meat would offend the gods and the buddhas. The British expeditions held fast to this rule of non-violence, and those who were involved described later how tame the animals and birds were. Many hermits made their homes in caves in Chamlung, meditating, praying and searching within themselves for understanding and enlightenment. At around 16,000ft (4,876m) the monastery, which had been established by Dzatrul Rinpoche in 1902, was the highest in the world and was home to over 300 monks. It was an important goal for many pilgrims in southern Tibet, some spending months travelling there, prostrating their bodies full length as they went, carrying offerings of cloth, barley and yak butter, and seeking merit and blessings.

At Rongbuk Monastery, with the great chorten on the left.

Maurice Wilson wrote enthusiastically of visiting the monastery. 'The colour & décor & alive effects of the place are very charming.' Of the monks he commented 'What a good natured crowd.'

Although his diary does not give any more detail, I imagine that their blessing, probably in one of the monastery's small inner shrine rooms, was lively, with as many of the monks as possible crowded in, cheerfully pushing and jostling, curious to see the English stranger who had come so far. It was quite dark, the only light coming from low burning butter lamps and a half open door, and the air was a thick heady mix of powerful, unfamiliar smells – incense, sandalwood, dust and the slightly rancid smell of melting butter. Once their eyes had adjusted to the gloom they could see two lines of red wooden pillars, rows of wide, low benches for the monks, and a painted ceiling above, red picked out with flowers, birds and dragons all twisted together in geometric patterns, the colours rich and bright despite a fine, sooty film. Dignified in saffron and maroon robes, Dzatrul Rinpoche presided at the front, sat cross-legged on a raised dais before a polished figure of Buddha Shakyamuni. The Buddha was similarly sat on his lotus throne, the fingers of one open hand stretching downwards to show his connection with the earth, as images of other enlightened beings stood beside him in silent attendance. Gold, silver and precious stones gleamed as scores of moving flames flickered and danced, and thin threads of perfumed smoke drifted gently up from bunches of incense sticks, circling the holy statues before fading into emptiness. The monks shuffled and whispered to each other until a blast of drums, cymbals and horns announced the start of the ceremony.

The visitors moved forward in turn to the head lama. Tewang and Tsering prostrated full length first, and then bowed low in front of his dais, hands together and pressed to their foreheads. Keeping their eyes down they held out silky white khatas (prayer scarves) and their offerings. These were taken by one of the attendant monks, and Dzatrul Rinpoche leaned forward to touch each man gently on the crown of his head with a heavy silver dorje (the ceremonial thunderbolt, symbolising enlightenment). Then he returned their khatas, carefully draping them around their necks and quietly speaking blessings, and prayers for their spiritual progress. Maurice Wilson also presented his gifts, a blanket scarf and 5 rupees, and was blessed.

As most visitors to Rongbuk, Maurice Wilson was impressed by Dzatrul Rinpoche, who at over 70 years was already a great age for a Tibetan. Indeed he sensed that the feeling was mutual. They talked through an interpreter for half an hour, the other monks enjoying the translation, and posed together for a photograph. Maurice Wilson's diary records that Dzatrul Rinpoche 'was delighted when I told him I had travelled the world & never felt so happy in anyone's company before'. The two men agreed to eat together when Maurice Wilson got back. The monastery's return gift to the little expedition was a dish of barley meal and half a dried goat. Beaming broadly, Maurice Wilson showed the monks how he would use his small shaving mirror to let those down at Rongbuk know how he was getting on, noting, 'All lamas will be on lookout for my signals day & night so that progress will be known.' Eric Shipton later considered, 'He had evidently made a good impression upon the old man, who, when we visited the monastery in 1935 talked to us a good deal about him.'[2]

That night, writing in his sleeping bag, Maurice Wilson was cheerfully optimistic, planning to reach the Ruttledge expedition's Camp II or III the following day. 'Gorgeous sunset on E tonight & feel it heralds success.' It was very cold, and he only slept fitfully, in the strange dreams of altitude perhaps picturing a triumphant return to Rongbuk, the monks waiting to greet him, led by Dzatrul Rinpoche with his all knowing smile and kind brown eyes.

The following day, Monday, 16 April 1934, Maurice Wilson rose early, left camp at dawn and strode away alone, his chin set firm and his eyes looking ahead towards Everest. It was a perfect morning, with a pale sky slowly changing from silver to blue, and hardly a breeze moving the air. At this stage the walk was relatively easy. Leaving the monastery there is a route through the rough moraine, where great lumps of rock are piled in haphazard heaps with smaller stones between. The river runs to one side, and on the other is a rise up to the lower slopes at the edge of the Rongbuk valley. Here and there green cushions of saxifrage cheer the otherwise barren looking boulders, prayer flags are tied to bundles of sticks, and chortens and mani stones mark bends in the path.

On the higher slopes there are amazing rock formations – strata of grey, brown and sandy yellow stone, twisted and thrust so sharply upwards by the forces of the earth that their stripes run almost vertical in places, and have been carved by ice and wind into natural ramparts and turrets. Beyond them the outcrops are dusted with snow and, higher still, there is thick glacier ice, with sharp black rock ridges breaking up the white, and outlining the mountains. As clouds march across the sky, different snow slopes and peaks are touched by sunlight, seeming to stand out more vividly than their neighbours. Watching the mountains the view changes constantly; a never-ending procession of the elements. It is a vast, magnificent, almost cathedral like landscape to walk through, quiet but for the harsh cries of ravens and the constant sound of the river, and on a day when the cloud is high the evocative mass of Everest is always in view at the end of the valley. The sheer North Face is flanked on one side by the North East ridge, which drops away from the summit, and on the other by the steep North West ridge, its length emphasising the height of the mountain. By day the bright sun makes it surprisingly hot walking; Maurice Wilson would not yet have needed his Yorkshire wool.

Feeling strong, despite the load he was carrying (over 45lb or 20.4kg), Maurice Wilson marched past the site of the Ruttledge expedition's base camp at 16,500ft (5,029m), just at the lower tip of the Rongbuk glacier, pausing briefly to admire the view, cool down and catch his breath. By then the sun was high, and I imagine at that point, flushed with his success so far, it would have been easy for him to feel he could climb Mount Everest. From there, around five miles (8km) past the monastery, the line of the valley beckons towards beautiful snow slopes beyond tumbled boulders, and someone believing it was meant to be might feel the climb was neither too far nor too hard.

Maurice Wilson's route was the one planned during the 1921 reconnaissance expedition. George Mallory and Guy Bullock, exploring the glaciers on the northern side of the mountain, had worked out that there was a way up from the head of the East Rongbuk glacier onto the 23,000ft (7,010m) North Col on the mountain's North East ridge, and from there to the North East shoulder and along to the summit beyond 'for anyone who cares to try the highest adventure.'[3] Maurice Wilson's sights were set on 'the highest adventure'; his target date for reaching the top was 21 April, his 36th birthday.

In the harsh sun he marched on through the rocky moraine fields, following a track at the side of the glacier that had been pioneered in 1921, and followed in hope by each expedition since. Every now and then he stopped to check his height recorder. By three o'clock Maurice Wilson had climbed eight miles (13.5km), to around 17,600ft (5,364m), and was only about three quarters of a mile from the 1933 expedition's Camp I. He decided to camp there, on a level patch of moraine, sensibly giving himself enough time to get his tent up and Tommy stove going before the sun began to disappear behind the mountains, and the debilitating cold and dark set in.

   Although he had not got as far as he had over ambitiously planned the day before, Maurice Wilson seemed pleased enough with his progress, and he brewed a mug of tea and settled down for the night. I imagine him climbing into his sleeping bag, feeling quietly sure that his God, and the gods and goddesses of the mountains, were supporting him. After his day of leisure at Rongbuk, his diary returns to shorter, more focussed entries, but his words remain optimistic and confident. 'We're off & have got a good start as I'm only about three-quarters of a mile mile from Camp I. Hope to get to Camp III tomorrow & shall be happy. Am carrying terrific load.' 'Altitude easy.' 'Am just about nodding off to sleep as I was too damned cold to get any last night at Rongbuk.'

The chief Lama of Rongbuk, 1922. Photograph courtesy of the Royal Geographical Society.

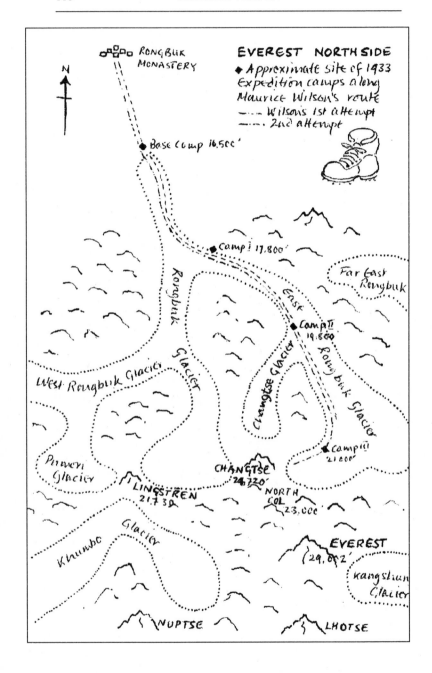

⚜ ⚜ ⚜ ⚜ ⚜ ⚜ ⚜

Tuesday, 17 April saw the first winds of change. To get to Ruttledge's Camp II Maurice Wilson had to follow the East Rongbuk glacier to a point roughly 2,200ft (670m) higher than his 16 April campsite. He rose early, but was delayed warming water for his breakfast tea and oats. More than ever appreciating Rinzing's care of their daily campfires, he impatiently spent the best part of an hour boiling a pot of water. Even when it bubbled promisingly, the temperature was so low he could put his hand in without any pain. It was well after dawn before he had eaten, packed up and set off.

After a while he reached the remains of Ruttledge's Camp I, at the point where the main Rongbuk glacier and the subsidiary East Rongbuk glacier meet, and found it reassuring to know he was on the right track. But from there the route was unclear and elusive, and to make matters worse Maurice Wilson had no experience of glaciers. As the ice got thicker and higher, it must have been daunting. But he had come through so many daunting experiences since he had left London that I imagine he simply squared his shoulders, took a deep breath and got on with it.

He plodded along, keeping as much as he could to either the moraine ridges at the glacier edge, or to the bottom of channels between walls of ice. This meant he could walk fairly easily along the loose stone, passing between seracs and cold meltwater pools, but he frequently got lost and had to double back on himself. It was hot, the sun was relentless and his breathing was an effort, especially in the troughs, where the air felt stagnant and still. It was a weary, miserable slog with every step an effort for mind and body. But Maurice Wilson was strong and fit, and his determination kept him going. He unpacked some things from his heavy rucksack and abandoned them. Although he did not cover anything like the distance he had hoped, in the circumstances he did well to continue gaining height that day, and to keep heading in more or less the right direction.

It is easy to appreciate some of his feelings that night from the words of his unusually low-key diary entry, which say little but somehow convey so much. 'What a hell of a day on Rongbuk glacier. No track to be seen & have been floundering about doing 50 times more work than needed.'

The following day, Wednesday, 18 April, was similar. 'Been a hell of a job again,' Maurice Wilson noted that afternoon, munching a slice of bread as he wrote. 'Shall not be able to make top on birthday unless a miracle happens.'

Despite the difficulty, he had managed to make progress and reached Ruttledge's Camp II (19,800ft; 6,035m), putting up his tent around four o'clock. He scouted around the remains of the expedition's camp, reporting seeing labels from tin cans but, disappointingly, 'not a cigarette butt to be found!' Everest towered above him, dominating everything, the relentless wind on the upper slopes whipping snow off the high ridges and running it over the mountain's shoulders like a gossamer shawl.

It is not surprising that Maurice Wilson preferred a bit of bread to the toil of cooking. At nearly 20,000ft (6,096m), everything is hard work, and food is unappetising. Slowly melting pots of snow for soup or tea is a chore after a day struggling on the mountain, and even members of recent expeditions, with a greater understanding of the importance of drinking enough at altitude, write of forcing themselves to stay awake long enough to melt snow, watching their camping stoves for an hour before each mug full, and then struggling to eat, despite all the calories burned every day. When up so high, there is almost no energy, strength or will to spare.

Perhaps without realising it, Maurice Wilson also

described another classic effect of altitude – of anything extra being too much trouble. 'The glaciers are marvellously beautiful,' he wrote. 'Gorgeous duck egg blue. Too tired to take out camera, but will get them on way back.' Extreme height exhausts both the mind and the body. People can become confused, depressed, argumentative and emotional. In his account of the 1922 expedition, John Noel noted that George Finch, who was an enthusiastic photographer and desperately wanted to take pictures of the upper slopes of Everest, did not even take his camera out of its bag on his world record climb up to 27,300ft (8,323m), because 'he could not be bothered.'[4]

But, despite the altitude, Maurice Wilson continued to write a little in his notebook each day. I wonder if he found it a comfort. A way of keeping his spirits up, of communicating with friends at home and a statement of his faith. If his destiny and task were to climb Everest then, if necessary, a miracle would come. 'Saw E in snow & mist just this pm. What a gorgeous sight.'

On Thursday, 19 April, things got worse. Beyond Camp II, there is less rock moraine, the ice towers and ridges crowd together, and Maurice Wilson found it almost impossible to work out a way through. Although he had read about the 1920s expeditions, the accounts, which had been written by mountaineers for members of the public, understated both the frustrating maze of the East Rongbuk glacier and the technical difficulty of getting up onto the North Col. After all, with climbing experience, crampons and rope, members of those expeditions had beaten a path beyond it, and the stories to tell back home were of the challenges and adventures on the upper slopes, not of the achieveable difficulty in getting there.

Without pictures it is hard
to visualise the size and
scale of the East Rongbuk
glacier, or to empathise with
Maurice Wilson's predica-
ment. The glacier is a frag-
mented sprawl of icebergs, a
bewildering maze of spires
and skyscrapers of ice, each
one higher than a house and,
from the base, impossible
for a man to see over. There
are fantastic frozen formations, and sunshine creates
illusions with light and
shade. Rocks and stones are
suspended in the ice, and
spectrums of milky blue and
green glint within it.
Constantly shifting, freezing
and melting in turn, it
groans and cracks eerily.
The glacier moves, slowly
but surely, always changing;
its weight and power shap-
ing the landscape as it goes,
scratching grooves into rock
in one place, and dumping
boulders at the next. In photographs of the early expeditions, lines of men, roped
together, are dwarfed by it,
and their tents look tiny.
Some stony ribbons and
ridges of moraine suggest a

Ice pinnacles of the East Rongbuk Glacier. Photograph courtesy
of the Royal Geographical Society.

way through, but they are as uncertain as sheep tracks, good for a while but then ending in a cul-de-sac, so that you have to retrace your steps and look for another way, cursing and dispirited.

In his account of the 1922 expedition, John Noel described how the team's Sherpa porters established a series of camps up the mountain. The second, which he called Frozen Lake Camp, was at 19,500ft (5,944m) and the third, Snowfield Camp, was at 21,000ft (6,400m).

Noel wrote: 'Between Frozen Lake and Snowfield Camps the glacier was twisted and broken into a belt some two miles wide of broken, splintered bergs of ice, some towering to a hundred feet in height. Here the men would strap steel spikes to the soles of their boots and set out along one of the strangest paths imaginable. They would find their way, turning and twisting in every possible direction, past the towers and pinnacles of ice, avoiding fissures fifty feet deep, descending walls of ice a hundred feet in depth, following old widened crevasses, climbing ladders that we cut in the ice, guided by a line of little flags we fixed to wooden pegs hammered to the tops of ice hillocks. These showed the way when storms and mists concealed the more distant landmarks and snow covered the foot tracks. We named this region 'The Fairyland of Ice'. Actually it had been a work of many days to discover a path by which to penetrate the maze. Bergs and cliffs and crevasses blocked the way a dozen times to the first exploring party, and were circumvented only by retracing steps and starting afresh from some new direction.'[5]

Following his 1980 climb Reinhold Messner also wrote of passing through the glacier, on the way up to his advance base camp below the North Col. 'On the third day after leaving base camp we continue on our way along the central moraine which has melted a trough between the walls of the glacier. So we pass between icebergs, séracs, ice walls. In Tibet not only the clouds change in the wind, but also the mountains, the hills, the ice. I can literally see that this high plateau is alive like the sea, that it smells like hide, that it vibrates like a sea of lava.'[6]

Doggedly Maurice Wilson kept going, slipping on the ice when forced off the moraine and putting his faith in the paths he found, self-discipline making him put one foot in front of the other, despite his exhaustion. It started to snow about an hour after leaving Camp II, which added to the difficulty of finding a route, and he was very thirsty, stopping to eat snow and ice to try and ease his dry, rasping throat. Depressingly he camped only three-quarters of a mile (1.2km) beyond Camp II.

The following morning, Friday, 20 April, he plodded on again, grateful for the previous day's snow as it meant the ice was less slippery, but still without a good route through the glacier. 'Am on wrong side of it, but must be a way round somehow.'

Maurice Wilson was desperate to reach Camp III because his food supplies were running dangerously low. The Sherpas had told him there was a ration dump left by the Ruttledge expedition about half a mile (0.8km) from the camp. He had hoped to be within striking distance of the summit by 20 April, and provisioned accordingly. Now he wondered whether having more to eat might solve his dragging weariness. 'Still about two and a half miles to go to Camp III, when shall look forward to some hot chocolate,' he wrote, once his tent was up after another day of painfully slow progress and many dead ends. Surprisingly he noted that he didn't 'feel any ill effects' before adding, perhaps a little enviously, 'Think the climbers had it cushy with servants & porters.' At this point his camp must have been at around 20,500ft (6,248m).

❄ ❄ ❄ ❄ ❄ ❄ ❄

Saturday, 21 April was Maurice Wilson's birthday. He made two entries in his diary.

'36 today. Many happy returns to myself. Had hellish cold feet all night. Sun is just up so am finishing breakfast & shall have a little sleep.'

It sounds like he was starting to suffer from a terrible fatigue and lassitude, and the numbing, debilitating mountain chill that slowly and dangerously creeps through limbs and into the very core. Curling up in his tent must have felt so much easier, and more appealing, than going on, struggling to breathe, willing his feet to move and fighting unshared and crippling doubts.

As it was, when he finally managed to summon the energy to bundle up his tent and belongings, he did not get far. 'Overtaken by snowstorm and parked early.'

By this point it is a testament to his strength that he was able to put his tent back up, at least well enough to give him shelter against the snow. He must have been exhausted, his weak left arm was painful and he would only have been getting about half the oxygen we are used to at lower altitudes. Any effort would have meant the hammering of heart and lungs. It was not the birthday Maurice Wilson had dreamed of.

That night he took stock of his situation. He was cold, utterly worn out, despondent, and short of food and equipment. He was dehydrated, and the glare of sunlight on ice had left his eyes burning and painful to open, as though they were full of sand. 'Eyes terrible & throat dry.' Although he blamed the latter on keeping his mouth open in the wind, given the height he was at, Maurice Wilson cannot have been drinking enough. He could risk going on, relying on finding

Ruttledge's Camp III and the supply dump beyond it; but he had been trying to reach Camp III for the best part of four frustrating and depressing days without success. Or he could go back, recover, re-provision and try again.

Ultimately Maurice Wilson wanted to get to the top of Everest, and despite his weariness, the deluding effects of altitude on his mind and the attraction of dozing the hours away in the relative comfort of his sleeping bag, he was sensible enough to realise that his best chance was to go back to Rongbuk. All the previous expeditions had needed more than one attempt.

His record of the following day noted, 'Discretion better part of valour & with even Herculean effort could not make Camp III in time. Weather bad.'

He put together a small rucksack for his return – 'flea bag, tent and short rations' – and took advantage of a break in the weather to start his journey. Fortunately he remembered enough of the route through the glacier to be able to avoid the wrong turnings and paths that had taken so much out of him on the way up, and he managed to get almost back to Camp II before setting up his tent on the glacier for the night.

※ ※ ※ ※ ※ ※ ※

Having eaten only a slice of bread, he began again at six o'clock the following morning, Monday, 23 April, sucking snow and ice in place of a drink. Somehow, probably through desperation, he found a reserve of strength or adrenalin, for he travelled helter-skelter all the way to Rongbuk that day, arriving at the monastery at ten o'clock in the evening. The same distance had taken him three days on the way up. When he wrote his diary up later he commented, 'Turned out more energy today than in any week of my life.'

Maurice Wilson's race back down the mountain, descending over 4,000ft (1,219m), was a remarkable feat, showing how physically tough he must have been, or perhaps that a divine force truly was looking after him. The going was not easy, and it can be harder climbing downhill than up. But he hurried, skidded and slid, hardly pausing to catch his breath or collect more ice to suck to ease his throat, oblivious to both his own pain and the majesty of the mountains around him.

Although the weather had lifted, the snow that had fallen over the last few days had blanketed the grey moraine in white, making it treacherous underfoot and difficult to tell which boulders were stable and which were not. He was half blind, his eyes red and gummed up, his throat was sore, his legs wobbly, his body bumped and weary, and his left arm almost useless. Recalling it he wrote, 'If stumbled just had to let myself go, roll over & scramble on again.' Perhaps he was half delirious, for his mind was full of his friendships back home, and thoughts of his mother, his pencil confiding that their love was 'the only true romance I've ever had in life.' 'Am going to take her round all the old childhood spots when I get back.'

He hurried past the site of Camp I, not daring to stop, and then down to Ruttledge's base camp, beyond the end of the two Rongbuk glaciers. Away from the ice the going should have been easier, but the sun had set and it was quickly getting very cold and dark. Limping and aching Maurice Wilson staggered on, unbelievably walking for four hours just by the light of a new moon. The Rongbuk valley is so rocky that he must have tripped many times, no doubt ricking his ankles and further bruising his already battered body. Although light-headed he found the desperate strength to keep going and finally found himself near the monastery, calling out weakly for help.

Although Maurice Wilson was a self sufficient man, happy with his own company, his description of meeting his Sherpa guides shows how alone, tiny and isolated he had felt on the mountain, and how, in the last couple of cold, dark nights in his tent, he had missed the warmth of human contact. For me, these words are some of the most moving and personal in his diary. Tewang, 'rushed with outstretched hands and a row of snow white teeth in a smiling face. Next came Tsering in thick night attire, also with a glad smile, followed by Rinzing.' 'All delighted.'

Gently the three Sherpas took Maurice Wilson's rucksack from him and helped him into one of the monastery guest houses, which were used by pilgrims and travellers. They rolled out his sleeping bag next to a fire, and settled him into it, pulling as many blankets and rough sheepskins as they could find round and over him. They built the fire up with dried yak and pony dung and hurried to the kitchen for supplies. 'Then the food,' he recalled, 'rice, soup, fried Tibetan meat and the most gorgeous pot of tea I ever had in my life'.

A BREAK AT RONGBUK

*He who approaches close must ever be led on, and
oblivious of all obstacles, seek to reach that most
sacred and highest peak of all.*

Noel Odell

Not surprisingly, it took Maurice Wilson some time to recover from the rigours of his first attempt on the mountain. Strong and fit though he was, he must have used almost all his physical and mental reserves. He spent the first three days in bed being cared for with patience and gentle kindness by Tewang, Rinzing and Tsering; mostly sleeping but also watching his Sherpa companions as they went about their chores, and listening to the low, steady chanting of the monks at prayer, punctuated by the long, mellow sounds of their horns, which echoed around the valley. On Tuesday, 24 April, 'Spent all day in bed & ATE. Eyes terrible, sore & red.' He knew he was fortunate to be alive, and to have escaped without either frostbite, or more severe snow blindness. Others had attempted the mountain and not been so lucky.

Whether through arrogance, stupidity, gritty single mindedness or complete faith Maurice Wilson did not take his survival as a warning. Instead, in the comfort and easier altitude of Rongbuk, he held fast to his determination to try again, recording in his diary entry for Tuesday, 24 April, 'It is decided that Tewang & Rinzing will go to Camp III with me after a few days, where I shall rest for a while, then make a dive for the last stretch, & they will await my return & all come back together. There is plenty of sensible food up there.' (Once they had reached Tibet, Tsering had struggled with the altitude more than anyone else in the group, suffering with headaches and dizziness. He could not acclimatise properly at Rongbuk, and would not have been able to climb any higher.)

Having agreed his plan with the Sherpas, Maurice Wilson resigned himself to waiting until he was strong enough to make a second attempt, settling down to what sounds to have been something like a holiday stay within the monastery complex. Instead of using their tents, he rented a couple of guest houses for the four of them. (He described these as 'bunglas' in his notebook, possibly taking this from the Hindi 'banngla', meaning house.) Traditionally Buddhist monasteries in the Himalayas offer simple accommodation to pilgrims, visitors and travellers.

During his slow recovery, Maurice Wilson's diary recorded his day-to-day activities. 'Had lovely bath in a basin in bungla adjoining cookhouse & have had lunch sitting up for a change.'

'Eyes much better. Another couple of days should see me on the job again.' He spent time with Tewang, Rinzing and Tsering, enjoying their cheerful, easy company. 'Sat in boys' bungla all day yesterday for a change.'

His spirits restored by warmth, food and companionship, Everest's hold over Maurice Wilson strengthened again, drawing him to look up the valley, recording the weather on the mountain, making plans and analysing what might improve his chances of success. He experimented with biscuits made out of broken up bread and Quaker oats – 'surprisingly good' – optimistically thinking he would use them at Camp V and above. 'Much handier than bread.' He seemed to gain confidence knowing there would be someone to look after him at least part of the way up, noting, 'Used to forget to eat food on the job as I was never the least bit hungry.'

Maurice Wilson's recuperation at Rongbuk coincided with one of the many Buddhist festivals. He did not mention which one it was, and probably did not know, referring to it as 'some cheroo', but it must have been a colourful sight as the monastery was overwhelmed with pilgrims and other visitors. He reported that a small market was set up for a few days in the shelter of Rongbuk's walls, for the Tibetans are great traders, and at festival time there is feasting, a ready market for trinkets and people wanting food, yak butter and other items as offerings. The wares were laid out in colourful piles on blankets and cloths spread on the ground – tough whiteish cubes of dried yak cheese strung together; a few vegetables; dried fruit; blocks of black Chinese tea; gemstones, beads and silverware. He wrote on Monday, 30 April, a cold and cloudy day, 'Went to bazaar just outside monastery & bought supply of sugar & dates. Caused great excitement. They are a very good natured crowd & always smiling.'

I imagine Maurice Wilson found seeing the festival, and the people it brought to the monastery, a vibrant and unique experience. Having kept a low profile while they travelled through Tibet, he had not had any real contact with the local people. Now, perhaps feeling that his time on the mountain or his status as a guest of the monks, somehow protected him from the dzongpen's authority, he had both the confidence and the opportunity to mix with Tibetan people; although he would have been an object of curiosity himself, inviting hidden stares, nudges and shy smiles. A seemingly endless trail of people walked and prostrated clockwise round the outside of both the gompa and the big, white chorten, reciting mantras and spinning prayer wheels, so sending prayers for the enlightenment and happiness of all beings into the wind, to be carried to the four corners of the world.

At the bazaar, men and women mingled together in easy, light-hearted groups, talking, bartering, and exchanging news, dressed in their best for the event. Children and dogs

The Rongbuk Valley - cloud clearing in the morning.

pushed their way through a crowd of legs, while chickens pecked in the dust hoping for scraps, although they often lost out to the scavenging gorak (ravens). Helping wild creatures brings merit, and the Tibetans believe that gorak are psychic, and messengers of the gods.

The women wore ankle length robes with loose sleeves and high necks, had striped aprons tied around their waists, and beads and silver jewellery hung from their necks. Their long dark hair either stretched down their backs in heavy plaits, or was wound up and decorated with elaborate head-dresses, or semi precious stones and beads, they had long ear-rings of turquoise and coral, and carried strings of prayer beads in ivory, sandalwood or bone. The men's robes (chupa) were shorter, mainly ending just below the knee above colourfully embroidered felt boots. These were bunched and fastened at the waist with a belt, the front opening making a convenient pouch for keeping things – a silver hand prayer wheel, wooden bowls for food and drink, a knife, a flask of chang, or some twine. Many also had turquoise, coral or bone earrings and long pigtails, and wore strings of prayer beads around their necks. Most Tibetans prayed as they went about their daily tasks, running the 108 beads that make up a Buddhist prayer string almost unconsciously between their fingers as their lips mouthed familiar mantras.

In the 1930s, many Tibetans were herders, moving their animals – yaks, sheep, ponies and goats – from area to area looking for grazing. They took their homes and families with them, in large black yak hair tents, and no doubt there were a few near Rongbuk for the festival, the animals ambling peacefully nearby and smoke drifting up through a single hole in the middle of each tent roof.

By contrast, the pilgrims came with almost nothing, at most a bundle wrapped in a blanket carried on their backs, for Buddhists believe that a peaceful mind and progress along the path to enlightenment do not come with the possessions of this life. They journeyed to Rongbuk, and the holy Chamlung area, repeating prayers, prostrating as they travelled; hands pressed together, first touching the crown of their heads, then, in turn, their foreheads, throats and chests before stretching out along the ground as far as they could reach, standing up, moving forward a stride and repeating the movement, over and over, mile after mile, palms and knees protected by wooden blocks. Moving in this way over months, and sometimes years, along a holy pilgrimage route brings great merit.

Buddhism, more a way of being than a religion, was the essence of life in Tibet in 1934, as it had been for hundreds of years. In the monasteries and nunneries, those who were ordained studied holy texts, but ordinary people carried the core teachings and values in their hearts; pictures and statues of buddhas, bodhisattvas and great teachers stood on family altars with butter lamps and offerings, and parents and siblings supported as many family members in pursuing a monastic life as they could. As faith was an integral part of everyone's existence, a festival was a great reason to come together; a loud and joyous time for feasting and fun.

The monks, after their pujas and prayers, presented masked dances to the crowd. In a country where few needed to read or write, these gave lessons in impermanence, the risks of hate, greed, harming others and attachment, and of the certainty of death. The steps began slowly and were carefully choreographed, but as the tempo of drums increased they became dizzyingly wild and furious. There was a din of clashing cymbals and deep blasts from conch shell trumpets. The monks twisted, jumped and scampered, their brocade robes, headdresses and precious stones flashing rich rainbow hues. Smells of incense and juniper, themselves offerings to the mountain gods, hung in the air. The enormous wooden masks (which Maurice Wilson described in his diary as 'horrendous') were ornately carved and painted, bright representations of animals, skulls and the faces of both guardian protectors and fierce wrathful deities. With the cymbals, drums and horns, growing faster and louder, the monks spun to a climax in a frenzy of colour, passion and sound.

Then everyone tucked into a feast – meat, tsampa moistened with yak butter or tea and rolled into balls, eggs, momos (dumplings filled with meat or vegetables), yak cheese, eggs, chang (rice spirit) and millet beer. Savoury smells began to overpower the incense, and the monastery complex was soon loud with voices, laughter and singing. Millet beer is instant, made from pouring hot water onto millet grains and then drinking it through a bamboo straw once it has started to ferment. Tewang, Tsering and Rinzing joined in cheerfully. 'Boys having millet beer,' Maurice Wilson

wrote. 'Made in bamboo about 30 inches long with handle &
plunger. They pump away about ten minutes in order to get
all the good from the millet.' He did not mention trying it, but
it can be very potent, especially at altitude.

Although the weather was not always kind at the end of
April and beginning of May that year, with cold winds and
the mountains often in cloud, it was good enough for Maurice
Wilson to be able to stroll down the valley, exploring the area
behind the monastery when he needed some space and time
to think, apart from the rumbustious festival crowds. He did
not write of needing it, but I imagine Chamlung offered him
sanctuary; away from memories of bullets and decaying
corpses, away from both sour failed relationships and unattainable love, and away from the hopes, conventions and
expectations of others.

Maurice Wilson was used to long days of walking, and to
get himself stronger he explored the Rongbuk valley, and the
lower slopes of its hillsides, clambering over rocks, striding
out when he found a track, sitting in the sun or enjoying the
breeze and watching the animals and birds. Out of respect he
avoided the small nunnery, set up on a rocky ledge, but he
passed the hermits' dwellings, using the same paths as those
that brought food and water to the holy men in their silent
retreat.

For all that it was blessed, Chamlung was a hard and barren place to live. Not only did those who took part in the first
Everest expeditions notice how tame the birds and animals
were, but they also wrote of how the wild creatures and the
hermits seemed to look after each other. The holy men would
say it arose from compassion, a wish to help others and a
recognition that people, animals, birds and insects alike are
suffering in the endless cycle of samsara, which traps all
beings as they move in a snakes and ladders journey from life
to life. When their natural fodder was scarce up on the glacier the bharal (the now very rare blue sheep) would come

down to the hermits' caves and take food by hand. In turn the bharal allowed choughs, who soared high and were tossed about by the mountain winds, to rest on their backs, picking off parasites and other insects caught in their wool. Mousehares stored grains in their burrows, always leaving a pile at the entrance for their neighbours, small sparrow-like birds. The little birds, camouflaged, like the mousehares, with a sandy dust colour repaid this kindness by acting as sentinels, calling an alarm whenever they caught sight of one of the hawks, which were their mutual predator.

On Wednesday, 9 May, Maurice Wilson spent a while looking around the outside of the gompa, reporting later in his notebook that he had 'caused much excitement amongst the lamas.' I wonder what they thought. To them, not only did his goal have no spiritual benefit, it was dangerous for he unnecessarily risked both the anger of the gods and his own death, squandering a rare and precious human life, which to a Buddhist gives the only real opportunity to make spiritual progress. But they were always warm, smiling their welcome and peaceful acceptance, and maybe they looked on him more kindly than members of the big, well-supported expeditions because he came quietly and alone.

For his part, Maurice Wilson was impressed by the links between the monastery and the surrounding communities. He noted, on Friday, 4 May, 'Lama sends bits of food to all people in locality. There seems to be a very sincere friendliness between lamas and folks in Tibet. Quite different from what have noticed elsewhere.'

Like the other buildings at Rongbuk, the gompa was low and painted white, with a broad strip of ruddy chestnut brown immediately below the lip edge of the flat roof. It had small windows with carved wooden frames, and a wide doorway, up several rough steps, the heavy door concealed by full length white cloth curtains, bordered in red and royal blue with the eternal knot symbol worked in finer blue cloth in the centre of each.

Circumambulating the square based chorten, with its great domed top and pointed gold crown, was an act of worship and a way to gain merit. Many times each day, pilgrims, local people and monks alike, walked or prostrated round it, always clockwise, generally praying but sometimes chatting, invariably followed by one or two of the dogs that live around every monastery.

Although Dzatrul Rinpoche had founded the monastery seen by the members of the early Everest expeditions, Rongbuk had been a holy site since the eighth century. Then Guru Rinpoche, perhaps the most important Himalayan sage, had travelled from India, at the invitation of Tibet's king, bringing Buddhist teachings with him. His first task had been to subdue the spirits and forces of nature, which underpinned the old Bon religion. During the months he spent in Chamlung, through the power of his mind and, as legend had it, by flying to the top of Chomolungma, Guru Rinpoche persuaded the old gods and goddesses of the sky, mountains and earth (including Miyolanagsangma and her fellow Long Life Sisters), to protect and support Buddhist dharma teachings. Consequently these gods and goddesses, each with their own special qualities and powers, were honoured by offerings of flowers and the scent of burning juniper or azalea leaves. In time they came to symbolise both the interdependence of the local people and their environment, and the Buddhist teachings of compassion and respect for all.

This was described in a little book written for pilgrims, a copy of which was presented by Dzatrul Rinpoche to members of the 1936 expedition. 'In Ron-phu-rdza Padmasambhava [the Sanskrit name for Guru Rinpoche] spent seven months and realised the highest siddhi [spiritual attainment]: he ordained the region to be a place of salvation to all who beheld, heard or thought of or touched it. At that time, in a place where the auspicious long-lived-five-sisters

(Bkra-sis-tshe-rn-mched-lna), whose esoteric name was Immoveable Good Cow (Mi-gyo-glan-bzan-ma) walked the earth, in view, namely of the high, self create, ice mountain named Lady Cow (Jo-mo-glan-ma), he exorcised Mi-gyo-glan and the others by his word and blessed the place to be a chief scene of siddhi.'[1]

Maurice Wilson did not mention going into the Rongbuk monastery, other than for his blessing by the abbot. However, John Noel, who explored areas of the Himalayas before the First World War, and then took part in the Everest expeditions of 1921, 1922 and 1924 wrote of having an irresistible fascination for it, describing it as a 'place of joy' and noting the laughter of the monks and their gentleness, particularly for all wild creatures. 'I can describe it best as a mixture of pious religion and uproarious laughter – and a little dirt.'[2]

He admired the holy books, stacked on shelves in the main gompa and smaller rooms leading off it. Then books were sacred in Tibet. The loose strip pages of traditional Buddhist texts, usually about twelve inches by three inches (30cm by 7.6cm) and painstakingly hand printed, are held between narrow pieces of polished wood and then wrapped in bright silk. Just looking at holy books with a virtuous mind can bring merit, and the devout will walk, bent double, under the lowest shelves to gain blessings from the papers and their teachings.

Although they were friendly, John Noel thought the monks at Rongbuk saw the Everest expeditions as a threat and an intrusion, both into the sanctity of the mountain and the valley, and into their study and prayers. After the 1922 expedition, in which seven Sherpa porters died, John Noel reported being shown a new fresco, painted on one of the monastery walls, 'half historic, half prophetic.' 'This extraordinary picture shows the angered Deity of the Mountain surrounded by wierd, wildly dancing Demons, White Lions, Barking Dogs and Hairy Men, and at the foot, speared through and through, lies the naked body of the white man who dared to violate the ice-bound tempest-guarded sanctuary of Chomolungma – Goddess Mother of the World.'[3]

Despite his outwardly cheerful acceptance of his stay at Rongbuk, Maurice Wilson's recovery took longer than he had hoped. Although he included some encouraging entries in his diary, 'Feet feel much better,' and 'Fit as can be,' there were also setbacks, particularly once the festival had ended, and the monks went back to their simple lives of reflection. Maurice Wilson's face became swollen; blisters developed on his hands, and his eyes gummed shut and were very sore. A bit shamefaced, he was grateful when the inhabitants of the next guesthouse moved on: 'Rather pleased as she used to mumble prayers all day long.' he wrote.

At the end of April, just as Maurice Wilson's eyes seemed to be getting better, Tewang, who was pivotal to his plans for a second attempt on the mountain, became ill. After several days Maurice Wilson noted that it must be dysentery, planning to give his companion a mixture of whisky and barley flour, although it sounds as though his stomach massages brought the Sherpa longer term relief. To make matters worse, a few days later poor Tewang's foot became infected and painful.

Maurice Wilson, who had tucked into Tibetan meat since his flight down the mountain, blamed his own woes on the food, although the length of time he had been at altitude must have added to the strain on his body. He changed his diet, sticking to barley meal, chapattis and biscuits, and, a few days later, reported feeling much better. He still had a 'face like a dried apricot,' and was desperate for both a hair-cut and a shave, although with only rough knives available, neither was possible. He had also run out of cigarettes and was 'chasing up butts.' In the circumstances, resigned to waiting a few more days, he continued to record the small events of life – what he had eaten, how he had slept, what the Sherpas were doing and how he planned to help them after they had all got safely back to Darjeeling, along with a few thoughts about the people at home. On Thursday, 3 May, having recorded sadly 'Tewang still crook,' he put, 'Made some marvellous biscuits,' and 'Had Yorkshire pudding for tiffin.' And then touchingly, on Thursday, 10 May after Rinzing had made a trip to what was left of the 1933 expedition's stores, 'Santa Claus been round' – 'a 7lb tin of mint bulls eyes.'

However, Maurice Wilson was fed up of inactivity, and feared the start of the monsoon. On Friday, 11 May, having reported that Tewang seemed better, he wrote, 'In any event, we're all tired of waiting so decided, come what may, we go tomorrow. Shall be glad to get the job over and get back to Darjeeling.'

A SECOND GO

Only those who will risk going too far can possibly find out how far one can go.

T S Eliot

Maurice Wilson, Rinzing and Tewang left Rongbuk first thing on Saturday, 12 May, 1934, walking briskly along the broad valley floor and hoping the exercise would warm them after a bitterly cold night. There had been no blessing from Dzatrul Rinpoche this time, but the almost ever present scent of burning incense mingled with the more earthy smoke of the morning fire in the monastery kitchen, and those monks who were not praying or meditating left off their tasks for a minute or two to watch the little party in the dawn light. With Everest ahead of them, early morning mist hanging on the lower slopes, and the summit pyramid rising high above, the three men must have looked very small and frail.

They set a good pace, for the going on the first stretch was relatively easy, and Maurice Wilson felt particularly fit, having been up to 20,500ft (6,248m) just a few weeks before. They marched past the site of Ruttledge's base camp just below the main Rongbuk glacier, pausing briefly to drink from a meltwater stream, and to look back the way they had come, at the isolated valley, their track between glacier dumped mounds of grey rock, and the sprawling complex of white monastery buildings, with prayer flags fluttering on the slope above. That was the way back to Darjeeling, and home. The path ahead was more uncertain.

Feeling confident of this part of the route, and glad to be

back 'on the job', Maurice Wilson was impatient to cover as much ground as they could that day. The three men shouldered their rucksacks and, scrambling on the loose rocks, found a reasonable path along moraine to the edge of the glacier. They were able to stride along it pretty well, picking out rocks that did not look too wobbly, and marvelling at the power of the ice, and the mass of boulders and smaller stones it carried, colouring the lower levels of the ice a dirty grey.

After seven hours walking, the three men reached the site of the Ruttledge expedition's Camp I, and put their tents up. They had climbed around 1,800ft (549m). Tewang was 'just about flayed out,' although Maurice Wilson praised him highly in his diary for carrying his share and keeping going after three weeks of illness. He also commented, 'Rin been terrific today.' The sun went down shortly after they had stopped, and within minutes it got very cold. Maurice Wilson sheltered in one of the tents, jotting down his diary entry, while Rinzing and Tewang lit a fire and boiled some water. 'Writing in mitts in the boys' tent as my pencil is like ice. The boys are getting ready evening meal. Only hot tea and we brought plenty of ready made chapattis with us.'

As soon as they had eaten he went to his own tent to try and get warm in his sleeping bag, but he had a bad night, complaining the following morning, 'Had no sleep. The damned tea was like soup and kept me awake all night.' It does not seem to have occurred to him that his insomnia might have come from the increased altitude, particularly as he noted that Tewang had also been up in the night.

※ ※ ※ ※ ※ ※ ※

Maurice Wilson continued his diary more optimistically, 'Just waiting for b'fast coming up. They are blowing away with the bellows. Gorgeous day.'

I imagine the three of them in the bracing morning air sat,

or perhaps stood stamping their feet and trying to ease the overnight frosty stiffness of their boots, cradling mugs of tea in their hands, and trying to take in the immensity of the surroundings, their spirits lifted by the sunshine.

On Sunday, 13 May, the three men continued to make good progress. Maurice Wilson had been able to look for a route between the steep ice walls while Rinzing and Tewang prepared hot drinks and food for their breakfast. The two Sherpas' previous experience was invaluable in finding the right path and negotiating some difficult stretches. Not being lost in the dispiriting maze of moraine troughs, Maurice Wilson found the glacier much easier to walk through, although underfoot the rock was loose and sometimes so unsteady that it was a frustrating battle between stepping forward and sliding back. He kept a look out for the crampons that he had found on his first climb and then discarded; at the time unwilling to add to the weight he was already carrying, and unsure if he would need to use them. However, he did not find them again, and later realised that throwing them away had been a costly mistake.

Ice towered around them, in places sculpted into fantastic shapes by the weather, and so high that their horizon was reduced to ice, grey rock and sky. The sun was strong and hot, burning the skin, and its glare was blinding. Above, the occasional chough called as clouds drifted past, and after a couple of hours of strong sun some of the ice began to melt, so that in places they could hear a steady drip, drip, drip. Rinzing's smiles and good humour cheered them along when their sides were heaving, their hearts pounding, and it was agonisingly tempting to rest just a bit longer than the few minutes they allowed themselves to catch their breaths.

They climbed a further 2,000ft (610m) that day. 'Here we are at Camp II after what seemed like a spring walk after my last effort,' Maurice Wilson wrote contentedly. 'The water is just on the boil for tea after about one hour's blowing.'

Rinzing had enough energy left after the day's exertion to leave camp and spend an hour or so out on the glacier hunting for the rucksack Maurice Wilson had abandoned during his wild flight down the mountain the month before. Amazingly, he found it, along with a jersey he had been promised for his efforts, returning to the two tents in triumph well after the sun was down and the others had settled into their beds, trying to keep warm. Then the little camp fell silent, and despite the cold and eerie creaks from the glacier ice they had a better night.

The following morning, Monday, 14 May, they were later leaving Camp II than they had intended, as it took so long to melt snow and boil enough water for their breakfast drinks and food. However, buoyed up by the good progress of the last couple of days, they strode out, Rinzing carrying the bulk of the load. Once again the two Sherpas' experience made all the difference, as they were able to lead the way into, and then along, a moraine trough that gave a good route through the glacier heading towards Changstse (North Peak). Although both the altitude, and the stagnant feel of the air in the trough, meant it was an effort to breathe and will their legs to keep moving, they plodded along steadily.

As they climbed further up the mountain, the ice pinnacles grew closer together, and seemed to stretch higher towards the sky, the upper parts gleaming pale blue and green in the sunlight, while slowly but surely, as the moraine first narrowed and then petered out, there became more ice than rock. Away from the shelter of the trough, the wind screamed with a vengeance, blasting snow down from the ridges above. It quickly got very cold, the air suddenly catching sharp in the backs of their throats. Ruttledge's Camp III (21,000ft; 6,400m) was just a little further on, a bleak, desolate spot on rocks, close under the cliffs below the North Col.

They had climbed 1,200ft (366m) that day, making camp just before dark. After three days of climbing poor Tewang was exhausted, almost falling into one of the tents as soon as it had been put up, too tired to go a single step further.

Despite his relief at having reached Camp III at last, Maurice Wilson's priority was to find the 1933 expedition's ration dump, which was roughly half a mile (0.8km) further on, at a point known as Camp IIIA. No doubt the thought of what it might contain had kept him going through the day's low points, for from his diary there seems to have been no thought of waiting until daylight the following morning to look for it. Instead, once Tewang had been helped into his sleeping bag, he and Rinzing went out into the darkness, the cold too intense to spend any time admiring the millions of pure white stars above them. 'Rintzie wouldn't go alone for some fool reason,' Maurice Wilson grumbled later in his diary. That high up the mountain, I wonder whether the Sherpa secretly feared wandering spirits after dark, or even Miyolangsangma's guard dogs, for the Tibetans say that to approach the throne of the gods is to court disaster.

Whatever the reason, it was forgiven in the euphoria of finding a stack of boxes – the Ruttledge expedition's supplies. The three men had a 'Santa Claus party' with 'plum jam, honey, butter (hadn't seen any for nine weeks), cheese, assorted biscuits, Bournville chocolate, anchovy paste, sugar, Ovaltine, Nestle's milk & other treasures from home. Too late & too cold to do any cooking. So had biscuits & choc & went to bed on that.' Unfortunately, while putting up his tent in the cold and gathering darkness, Maurice Wilson had not levelled the snow and rock under it properly, so giving him another uncomfortable and sleepless night.

The following day, Tuesday, 15 May, the three men stayed around Camp III. Tewang slept, drained by the effort of three days' hard climbing. Rinzing went off to raid another box of food and Maurice Wilson alternately gazed up at the North Col, squinting in the bright sun as he tried to work out a route, and comforted himself with the 'treasures from home.'

The way up to the North Col looks daunting. Gigantic ice blocks lie tumbled at its foot, with dizzyingly high and steep ice cliffs above, sliced through by dark crevasses. Beyond them are wide, pristine snow slopes, beautiful to look at but giving climbers a dangerous avalanche lottery on their way up to more ice, and then onto the ridge of the Col itself at 23,000ft (7,010m). I wonder what Maurice Wilson thought as he stood near Camp III and studied the mountain. He may not have realised it, but the climb up to the North Col is probably the most difficult and dangerous part of the route he was taking. He hoped to find the ropes and steps the 1933 expedition had painstakingly established, although a couple of days later he was to realise that the ropes had been torn out months before, tossed away by the punishing Himalayan weather, and the ice steps had been broken and eroded to nothing.

Maurice Wilson perhaps did not appreciate that the East Rongbuk glacier is moving comparatively fast, and that a route used one year will invariably be gone the next. With the benefit of hindsight it seems obvious that supplementing his flying training with some climbing lessons, in the Alps perhaps, would have stood him in better stead than his fitness marches between London and Bradford. As it was he had no crampons and did not know how to tackle snow and ice slopes. Could faith and courage make up for this dangerous lack of equipment and experience?

Following the 1922 expedition, John Noel wrote, 'To anyone standing below, the Ice Cliff looms so terrifying, so sheer with its walls of ice a thousand feet high, so threatening with its yawning crevasses, that it looks too terrible a thing ever to propitiate. But it has to be done. It is the only way to the summit.'[1]

If Maurice Wilson feared what he saw ahead of him he did not share those feelings with his diary. Instead he kept his journal entry typically light, noting what he planned to carry for the next leg and writing cheerful thoughts about his day. 'Eaten everything about the place today. Soup, Ovaltine & heaven knows what.' Then, 'You couldn't guess what I'm wallowing in as I write? A full box of King George chocs! The sun has let up – it must be 4.30 or so. R is making Ovaltine for the nightcap. I am in my flea bag & ready for a long sleep. Shall be off tomorrow if weather good. Alone for the final crack.'

In the event Maurice Wilson spent such a miserable night, with a thumping altitude headache, that he stayed in his tent the following day, noting only one sentence in his diary.

He also stayed in camp on Thursday, 17 May. The weather had set in, as it can in the Everest region in April and May – 'snowing like the devil & can only see 200ft,' he commented. Again he complained of a headache – 'Terrible when you can't put your head down for aching' – but he wrote a long diary entry, and so I think must have felt less miserable than he had done the day before, perhaps partly because Tewang reassured him that 'everyone suffers the same.'

Maurice Wilson resolved to set off again the following day provided the weather was fit. From his diary it seems he had abandoned his unrealistic ambition of taking a 'short cut' to get to to Camp V in a single day because it would have meant him making his own path through the ice instead of following the 1933 team's route. He had reduced his luggage to a minimum, even cutting up the map so that he only needed to carry the relevant part of it, much to Rinzing's amusement. He reported having eaten anchovy paste from Fortnum & Mason's, another delicacy from Ruttledge's supplies, writing that he wished he could have wirelessed home about it, to amuse those waiting for his news. Tewang was still suffering and it was kindly Rinzing who kept the camp going, cooking, melting snow and mending Wilson's gloves. With an eye for the useful he 'bagged' a 20ft (6m) bamboo mast that had somehow been transported up to Camp III by the 1933 expedition as firewood, saving himself the trouble of cutting it up by having one end on his fire and then pulling more of it on, bit by bit, as it burned away.

Describing a little of life up at 21,000ft (6,400m), Maurice Wilson wrote, 'We feed only twice per day. First around 6.30 – 7am when Rintzi comes along with smoked tea or Ovaltine. Then about half an hour later comes soup, meal, etc. Then 2pm up comes the same again, & that's the last for the day so far as hot foods go. Everything is smoked. He puts my plate inverted over the boiling pot and all the smoke gets inside the pot.'

Back in Darjeeling, Tewang reported that, while they were all at Camp III, he had advised Maurice Wilson against going on, warning that he might not make it. Despite his optimism and faith, Maurice Wilson was a pragmatic man, and wise enough to realise from Tewang's comments that the authorities could make things difficult for the three Sherpas if they returned to Darjeeling without him. Consequenly, on 17 May he wrote a brief letter to the Deputy Commissioner and gave it to Tewang, along with a roll of film. On 30 April, well before the three of them left Rongbuk, he had written out a deed of assignment, passing ownership of the pony to Tewang, 'for services rendered.' Mentioning it in his diary the same day he noted that the Sherpa had promised not to sell the pony but to 'keep if for Lhasa trip.' Maurice Wilson planned to keep the animal's bell, bought for it by 'the boys' (because of its habit of running away), as a souvenir.

Sadly the weather over the next three days did not improve. The three men mostly stayed inside, sheltering from the elements and dozing as hour after hour dragged. The biting wind thundered across mountain rock and ice, beating the snow into drifts and buffeting the camp as though it was some force unleashed by the gods against Wilson's arrogant ambition, whipping their little tents until the men must have wondered if they would be blown off the face of the mountain. George Mallory described the Everest wind flapping tent canvas as making a deafening noise like machine-gun fire, and I wonder how Maurice Wilson felt in the black darkness of night if the same thought crept into his dreams, transporting him back to mud, blood and nightmare days in France.

Eventually he set out again on Monday, 21 May. Although Rinzing insisted on waiting until he had brewed tea for them all, he agreed to accompany Maurice Wilson half way up to Camp IV. The plan was to use the 1933 expedition's route, but finding that their ropes and track were no longer intact, they had to cut fresh steps up the ice. Taking the lead, Rinzing showed Maurice Wilson how to use his ice axe, although the ice and snow below the North Col is probably the worst place to have to learn this new skill. Step cutting is a craft, and at altitude is hard work, with experienced climbers going in pairs, taking it in turns to make steps for about twenty minutes at a stretch to share the load.

John Noel described how this was done by the 1922 expedition, giving an idea of the scale of the ice cliff and the task of climbing it. 'The men had to cut about two thousand foot-steps in the ice, and fix over 300 feet of hand ropes, attached to wooden pegs driven into the ice, following a zig-zag course to avoid the dangers of avalanches. We had to take the risk of these avalanches, which we knew might crush us at any moment. Steps were cut two feet deep through the snow into the hard ice beneath.'[2]

For the first stretch, while the two men were together, Rinzing used Wilson's ice axe to make steps steadily up the cliff. He left it as late in the day as he dared before turning back, conscious that he needed to be at least nearby Camp III before it got dark to avoid a potentially fatal fall. I imagine it was difficult for the warm hearted Rinzing to leave his employer, for despite Wilson's single minded stubbornness there seems to have been a genuine bond between him and his

The North Col from Camp III.

Sherpa companions. And although he was a brave and self-reliant man, Maurice Wilson must have felt suddenly very alone, perhaps even a little abandoned, as he watched Rinzing carefully retreat down the steps he had cut. Knowing the Sherpa was returning to a fire and company surely emphasised that he was again on his own on Everest. I wonder how much his faith, and the conviction he had in his own destiny, comforted that very human sense of isolation. As usual his diary entry was brief and factual, with his feelings left unsaid. 'I parked soon after he left me as the sun was sinking low.'

The following morning, Tuesday, 22 May, bright sunshine lit up the vast panorama of snow, ice and crags of the peaks around him. At that moment, Maurice Wilson was higher than anyone else in the world, privileged with a god's view across the mighty Himalayas and, if he cared to look down, of the Rongbuk valley, leading away to lower foothills and the broad sweep of the earth brown Tibetan plateau in the shimmering distance beyond.

With grim determination, Maurice Wilson packed his tent and rucksack and again picked up a route towards the North Col. He made painfully slow progress, slipping on the snow and struggling clumsily with his ice axe, trying to form adequate steps, panting for breath with the effort of each one, his weak left arm throbbing painfully, his eyes blinded by glare from the snow and his head swimming. I imagine he felt sick and wretched, but somehow he battled on, slipping and scrambling, perhaps keeping going without even knowing why, his mind dulled by lack of oxygen and fatigue as though he was in a sort of moving coma.

Maurice Wilson wrote of the day, 'Terrific grade again, worse than day previous. Am parked up below the chimney of the expedition.'

Wednesday, 23 May proved to be even grimmer as Maurice Wilson struggled on to try and reach Ruttledge's Camp IV, which was on a ledge, about twenty feet (6m) wide, roughly 200ft (60m) below the crest of the North Col. Climbers from the 1922, 1924 and 1933 expeditions all found getting up to the North Col difficult, and they were experienced men who knew how to negotiate a route over ice and crevasses, cutting steps, risking finger and toe holds to shin up the narrow chimney, using rope ladders and crampons, sharing the hard work and discussing Everest's challenges. In the circumstances, the miserable panting effort of Maurice Wilson's solitary task seems impossible.

He failed to reach Camp IV again that day, putting his tent up in a precarious position on some snow when he was either too exhausted to go any further or realised the light was beginning to disappear. He spent the following day in bed, noting in his diary, 'Had a horrible job yesterday.' He was also without matches, and so had no means of making a fire or melting snow for a drink. The night before he had used the last of his supply to make a candle stand, perhaps finding the light was company in his tent, but the matches had got saturated with snow and candle wax. Unbelievably he still seemed both optimistic and resolute, writing, 'Had five dry biscuits yesterday a.m. & nothing since as there is nothing to have. Camp IV is somewhere within half a mile radius so should be on the eats again by midday tomorrow.'

But despite writing about his hope of finding supplies, sometime in the dark solitude of night Maurice Wilson realised that carrying on alone meant certain death. His only chance of reaching the summit of Everest was by getting the Sherpas to help him up onto the North Col and as far as Camp V. From there he thought it would be a comparatively easy stretch to the summit. Whatever effect the altitude had on Maurice Wilson's mind, his strength of purpose and determination were undiminished.

The following morning, Friday, 25 May, he rolled up his tent at first light and packed his rucksack, sucking handfuls of snow to ease his dry throat. Then he began his second miraculous flight down the mountain. Fortunately, despite the strong winds, most of the ice steps had remained intact and he picked his way down them as quickly as he could, anxious to get back to the food, companionship and shelter of Camp III. With reckless desperation he even slid down stretches, fortunately neither starting any avalanches nor hurting himself badly.

His diary entry reflected his pragmatic assessment of his position, 'Only one thing to do. No food, no water. Get back. Rintzie came to meet me and wasn't I glad.'

Maurice Wilson was exhausted and spent the following two days in bed, doing no more than note that fact in his diary, as though he could not summon either the mental will or the energy to write more.

THE LAST EFFORT

Faith is not faith that waivers when its prayers remain unanswered.

Maurice Wilson

Maurice Wilson had returned to Camp III little more than a walking corpse, desperately exhausted and dehydrated. As he lay curled in his sleeping bag cocoon, drifting in and out of an unreal world of disjointed dreams, Rinzing and Tewang looked after him, melting snow and encouraging him to drink mug after mug of tea and Ovaltine. They must have thought that this time he would finally see sense and call it a day. Every other expedition had done the same, and the monks had said that was how it would be, for no man should set foot on the summit – there was no shame in leaving Chomolungma unclimbed.

Meanwhile the wind tore round the two tents, flinging ice crystals and snow against the canvas, roaring incessantly and forcing the two Sherpas to battle against it just to stand upright. They understood how vulnerable the three of them were out on the mountain, realising now, if they had not done so before, that strong, brave and fit though he was, Maurice Wilson's climbing skills were almost certainly not adequate to get him to the summit. They were also conscious that each day they stayed at Camp III brought the monsoon closer, threatening them all with being engulfed by avalanches. For Rinzing and Tewang, returning to Rongbuk was the only thing to do.

If he had been able to draw solely on the logical and

conscious parts of his brain at that point, Maurice Wilson
might have accepted that the Sherpas were right. He could
have walked with them back to Rongbuk and then, after a rest
in the monastery's healing atmosphere, trekked back to
Darjeeling, caught a train through India and a boat back to
England. His family, friends and the press would all have
welcomed him as a hero for everything he had achieved over
the past twelve months.

But in his heart, or his soul, or wherever a man's true
essence is, that was not enough. He did not want five minutes of fame for having had a good try. He had a bold and
public statement of faith to live up to. And he did not want
to go back to a directionless life in England. He wanted to be
the first to make it to the top of Everest and return. 'When I
have accomplished my little work,' he had predicted, 'I shall
be somebody. People will listen to me.' He wanted to be
'somebody' forever. And so Maurice Wilson could not turn
his back on his task. If God wanted him to reach the summit,
God would give him enough strength and would show him
the way. Believing in miracles, anything is possible.

At 21,000ft (6,400m) it is often not the rational and thinking parts of the brain that are strongest. Maurice Wilson had
been at high and potentially damaging altitudes for a long
time, starved of oxygen, and physically and mentally
exhausted. He had been running on empty for longer than
most people can. Perhaps, wrapped in his sleeping bag, and
wearing two balaclavas to muffle the haunting screams of the
wind, he no longer thought from what someone else would
call a logical base. Perhaps he did not analyse why he had to
keep going, or why he needed to try again. What mattered
was that he knew he had to. For Maurice Wilson there was
no option but to go on.

Reinhold Messner described how he felt climbing the same
route, also alone, 46 years later. 'Up here life is brutally
racked between exhaustion and will power; self conquest

Chang La (North Col) Chimney, Odell & porters (1924 expedition). Photograph courtesy of the Royal Geographical Society.

becomes a compulsion. Why don't I go down? There is no occasion to. I cannot simply give up without reason. I wanted to make the climb, I still want to. Curiosity (where is Mallory), the game (man versus Mount Everest), ambition (I want to be the first) – all these superficial incentives have vanished, gone. Whatever it is that drives me is planted much deeper than I or the magnifying glass of the psychologists can detect. Day by day, hour by hour, minute by minute, step by step, I force myself to do something against which my body rebels.'[1]

When they brought food and drinks to his tent, Maurice Wilson desperately tried to persuade the Sherpas to climb with him as far as Camp V. In turn they argued that, without the support of a larger expedition team, anyone going further up the mountain to establish a higher camp would be risking their lives needlessly and would be certain to fail, that the monsoon would be on them in a few days and that it was prudent to go back.

It is impossible now to know what was said, and it may be that Maurice Wilson's exhaustion and mental state meant he could not fully take in what was discussed, or understand the Sherpas. By this time his handwriting was sprawled and his diary entries are disjointed.

On Monday, 28 May he wrote, 'Tewang wanted to go back but persuaded him to go with me to Camp V. This will be last effort & I feel successful. From Camp V it is less than one-mile to top.' Later he added, 'Strange but I feel there is somebody with me in the tent.'

In fact it was not so strange. Facing extreme physical conditions some people, even those who do not see themselves as particularly imaginative or fanciful, find that the line between what is real and what is not, is both thin and blurred. While Maurice Wilson and so many other young men were fighting in Europe, Ernest Shackleton led a team attempting to cross the Antarctic. He wrote later that he thanked providence for guiding himself and his two companions, first in a small boat and then by foot, as they sought help and a rescue ship for their main party, adding, 'I know that during that long and racking march of 36 hours over the unnamed mountains and glaciers of South Georgia it seemed to me often that there were four not three.' [2] Inspired by Shackleton's comment, T S Eliot reflected it in *The Waste Land*, observing to his companion, 'There is always another one walking beside you.' [3]

In the Himalayas, Frank Smythe had reported a similar experience as he climbed alone on the upper slopes of Everest the year before Maurice Wilson's attempt; the feeling that there was someone with him was so strong that at a point where he rested he broke his piece of Kendal mint cake in two, holding half out to his invisible comrade. Alone on the mountain in 1980, Reinhold Messner found that his rucksack and ice axe were his companions, urging him on, and he heard voices in the air, which he accepted as real. Chris Bonnington also described how, in the effort of the last stretch of his successful climb along the South Col route to the summit in 1985, he felt 'almost the physical presence of Doug Scott,' [4] sensing his friend's reassurance and encouragement. Many others tell similar stories.

It seems very unlikely that Tewang would have agreed to try and get up to Camp V. Even after his long rest at Camp III he would probably not have been strong enough to lead the way up to the North Col and beyond, and must have known that going back was the only sensible option.

In any event, Maurice Wilson prepared to leave the following day, packing up some food, spare jerseys, the Union Jack and his precious 'flag of friendship'. The next morning he added his rolled up tent and sleeping bag.

Maurice Wilson left Camp III alone on the morning of Tuesday, 29 May. He asked Rinzing and Tewang to stay for a few days, and then to go back to Rongbuk and wait for him there. Then he turned and, facing the mountain, once again tackled the route up to the North Col.

Provided the ice steps had remained intact in the punishing wind, he could well have made good progress back up towards the chimney that day, although it is impossible to say how far he got as his notes of Tuesday, 29 May are essentially illegible. The following day he simply wrote, 'Stayed in bed.'

On Thursday, 31 May 1934, Maurice Wilson made his last diary entry, typically optimistic and cheery. 'Off again. Gorgeous day.'

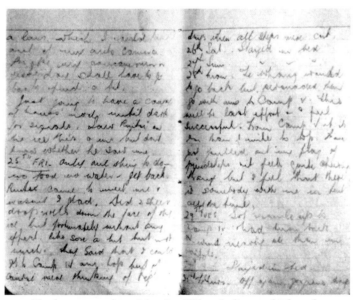

The last pages from Maurice Wilson's diary, which ends, 'Off again. Gorgeous day.'

THE FINAL CHAPTER

Have we vanquished an enemy? None but our-
selves. Have we gained success? That word
means nothing here. Have we won a kingdom?
No... and yes.
George Mallory

The news that Maurice Wilson was missing gradually filtered out in July 1934, when Tewang, Rinzing and Tsering returned to Darjeeling. Possibly afraid of the consequences, it seems they first reported that Maurice Wilson had caught a train at Kalimpong, bound for Calcutta, but from subsequent interviews it became clear that they had trekked back from Rongbuk without him, and believed that in all probability he was dead.

Tewang gave a matter of fact statement to the authorities, explaining how he had first met 'the Sahib' who had given him money to buy a pony from Kalimpong, and asked him to arrange porters. After a brief description of their march into Tibet, and Maurice Wilson's first attempt on the mountain, Tewang continued. 'He took rest for a few days and again left taking me and Rinzing. We went as far as Camp III. There he said he was going up to the top. I thought he would not be able to go and told him so. He insisted on going and I told him that he might die, in which case I and the two coolies might get into trouble on our return to Darjeeling. On my saying so he gave me this letter.' [1]

In his letter to the Deputy Commissioner at Darjeeling, Maurice Wilson explained that he had bribed the three Sherpas to take him to Rongbuk. 'They have served me faithfully through many tight corners,' he added, 'and I am asking you as a sportsman to use your endeavours to see that they go free from any punishment which certain civil authorities may consider it their 'Duty' to inflict.' Rather endearingly I think, the letter ends, 'Keep smiling and look after these lads. Cheerio.' [2]

Tewang's statement went on to explain that Maurice Wilson had asked he and Rinzing to wait for him for fourteen days, and that, if he did not come back within that time, to return to Darjeeling. Rinzing and Tsering had stayed at Rongbuk, while Tewang, still ill with dysentery, went a little lower to Chodzong to recuperate. After about two weeks Tewang said that the three Sherpas were running low on food and money, and so decided it was time to go back to India. Tewang asked Rinzing to talk to the monks at Rongbuk, to leave the five tins of Quaker oats (which were all that was left of Maurice Wilson's supplies) there in case he should need them 'and also to ask the lama to arrange sending the Sahib back to Darjeeling through some of his men.' [3]

Once again, Maurice Wilson's name, and his attempt to reach the top of Everest, featured in the newspapers. The *Daily Mail*, for example, reported on 20 July that he had 'lost his life at a height of 23,000ft,' continuing, 'On his gallant solo effort to beat the world's highest peak, Mr Wilson carried with him a light tent, three loaves of bread, two tins of porridge and a camera.' The article ends with, 'Yesterday came the news from Darjeeling that the gallant effort – which the Maharajah of Nepal had sternly forbidden the previous year when Mr Wilson wanted to fly over the mountain – had ended in tragedy.' [4] (The camera was never found.)

The following day the *Daily Mail*, in reporting that the Himalayan Club had offered to organise an expedition to search for Maurice Wilson if the government of India would meet the cost, said, 'Some of those who knew him intimately still have unshaken confidence in his ability to survive the dangers of starvation and exposure.' The piece added, 'The porters who returned without him only did so because they were on the verge of starvation, their food supplies being exhausted; but they seem to have profound faith in Mr Wilson's powers to survive, regarding him almost as a demigod. There is no doubt that they worshipped him as a born leader, and two of them have volunteered to join without payment any search expedition which is organised.' [5]

Given their strenuous efforts to stop him entering Tibet in the first place, it is not surprising that the Indian government did not take the Himalayan Club up on its offer. For the time being, Maurice Wilson's fate was left a mystery.

In a letter sent to the Political Officer in Sikkim the following month, Mr A McDonald Clark, Darjeeling's Deputy Commissioner, commented, 'I am afraid sportsmanship does not enter into a matter like this,' [6] but agreed that Tewang, Tsering and Rinzing all believed that their employer had permission to go to Everest, and that it would be pointless to prosecute them under the Bengal Eastern Frontier regulations.

The following year, 1935, the isolationist Tibetan government unexpectedly gave permission for a further expedition to the north side of Everest. Officially this was in recognition of Tibet's friendly relations with Britain and India, although at the time Major Williamson, the Political Officer in Sikkim, was told that ideally the Tibetans would have preferred there to be no expeditions at all as they brought trouble to the country. The notes he was given explained, 'the guardian deities of the mountain take great exception to such attempts and in their anger they render the weather very rough and the after-effects are very bad. Such attempts only work undesirably on the temper of the gods and guardian deities, which results in heavy snowfall and storm.' [7]

Despite these warnings, Eric Shipton was charged with leading another reconnaissance party. The joint committee of the Royal Geographical Society and the Alpine Club gave the team a cautious brief, not to attempt the summit but to look for alternative routes up to it from the west, to study the effects of the monsoon, and try out men and equipment that might be used for a later push for the top. Along with Eric Shipton, the group included Dan Bryant, Edwin Kempson, Charles Warren, Edmund Wigram, Michael Spender and Bill Tilman. Interestingly, the Sherpas that joined the group once they had reached Sikkim included Tewang, Rinzing and Tenzing Norgay. Having trekked across country from Darjeeling, the party left Rongbuk for the slopes of Everest on 6 July 1935.

Three days later, as they clambered across some moraine above Camp III, in search of the 1933 expedition's food dump, Charles Warren, who was climbing in the sunshine a little ahead of his companions, saw a boot lying in the snow, and a green mass just beyond it. 'Hello,' he shouted back to Eric Shipton, who had paused to sit on a rock, 'here is a perfectly good pair of boots and a tent; must be a dump.' But once he got closer he was shocked to find that it was a man's body, huddled in the snow, the other boot abandoned next to him. 'I say it's this fellow Wilson,' he shouted again. [8]

Charles Warren recorded in his diary that Maurice Wilson lay curled on his left side wearing a mauve pullover, grey flannel trousers and woollen underclothes, his legs were drawn up, and his feet were bare as if he might have been lying in bed. There was a stone next to his left hand, with the guy rope of a tent attached to it, suggesting that he might have been tightening it against the wind. His tent had been badly ripped by the mountain weather, and they pulled tatters of it out of the snow nearby. From the position of the body Charles Warren, the expedition doctor, concluded that

Maurice Wilson must have died in his sleep from exhaustion and exposure, with the tent blowing away later.

The two men waited for a few minutes for the others to reach them and, once they were all together, had a brief discussion about what to do. Before disturbing the body, they searched the area and eventually found a lightweight rucksack containing Maurice Wilson's personal belongings. Having kept back the Union Jack, his 'flag of friendship', his gold pencil, one or two knick knacks and, most importantly, his diary, Eric Shipton carried out a simple funeral service. The constant changing of the moraine near Camp III ruled out a surface burial so the little group wrapped the body in what was left of his tent and tipped it into a deep crevasse in the ice. Charles Warren later described how they 'slid the body into the depths where it immediately disappeared from sight. We all raised our hats at the time.' [9] Afterwards they built a small cairn at the spot where Maurice Wilson's body had been found, using his ice axe as a cross.

I imagine that the team found it a distressing and unsettling experience; indeed Charles Warren wrote that everyone was 'rather upset' confiding in his diary that the tragedy felt 'a little too near home.' [10] Even these days, when bodies in the snow are sadly not an unusual sight along the routes to Everest's summit, seeing them must pull climbers up short emotionally, a chilling reminder of the risks they face. But in 1935 the unexpected discovery of Maurice Wilson, whose ambition, at least regarding Everest, they shared, perhaps not only reminded the group of their own mortality, but left them wondering whether anyone would ever make it to the top.

Like Maurice Wilson the 1935 expedition travelled light and had minimum supplies, buying food on their journey when they could, and so they too enjoyed treats from the 1933 food dump. That evening they sat together, grouped under an overhanging rock, and, as the snow fell steadily and silently beyond their shelter, feasted on toffee, jam, cake and

Fortnum & Mason Carlsbad plums. As they ate, Edwin
Kempson read aloud from the diary, which he described as 'a
moving and gallant document, but marred by his unwarrant-
ed self confidence.' [11] 'His diary showed a strong streak of
superstition,' Edmund Wigram considered, 'and there seemed
to be throughout a certainty in the mind of the writer that he
was destined to climb Everest. His confidence was almost
unbelievable.' [12]

In his observations, Charles Warren thought it curious that
Maurice Wilson died only 200 yards from the 1933 food
dump, but I imagine there must have come a point when
going to get food felt like too much trouble. How much more
tempting to doze in a warm sleeping bag. He was used to
going without, would almost certainly have been dehydrated,
and probably had no appetite. He had noted after his first
attempt on the mountain that he had forgotten to eat. If not
mentally, he must have been physically spent by then.

Bill Tilman, a practical man of few words, recorded in his
brief entry for the day that the Sherpas 'seem quite unmoved
by Wilson's body. One took his boots.' [13]   However, a couple of years later, Hugh Ruttledge, writing of the 1935 expedition, applauded Shipton, Kempson, Warren and a team of
Sherpas for reaching the North Col on 12 July. 'It was a fine
performance,' he noted, 'accomplished not without difficulties other than those of the ground; for some of the Sherpas,
perhaps upset by the discovery of Wilson's body, refused
work on one day; and Shipton was forced to read the riot
act.' [14]   Maybe the Sherpas wondered if the old mountain
gods had spoken again and did not want to anger them further.

Neither Tewang nor Rinzing were there when Maurice
Wilson's body was found. Afterwards there was some con-
troversy over how long they had waited for him, and where-
abouts, as he had died so close to the good food supplies near
Camp III, with Tenzing Norgay in particular feeling that the

two men should have gone to look for him. Eric Shipton noted that the two men 'said they had waited a month for him at Camp III, which was clearly untrue for they would certainly have visited the food dump from time to time and would have found the body.' [15] Without doubt what he was told was at odds with Tewang's statement from the previous year, which talked of the men waiting lower down, at Rongbuk and Chodzong, for a little over two weeks.

Only three people know what really happened, how long the Sherpas waited and where, when Maurice Wilson decided to go back towards Camp III and with what in mind, and whether he even managed to get his tent up properly before crawling under the canvas. Members of the 1935 expedition agreed that his lack of experience and equipment meant the Sherpas had been right to refuse to go with him up to the North Col. Rinzing and Tewang were under no obligation to risk their lives further for their employer, who chose for himself to keep battling upwards. They warned him not to go on, but in a distant and tragic echo of 'Stop me? They haven't a dog's chance,' could not have forced the strong-minded

Press photograph of Maurice Wilson, as he left London for India

Maurice Wilson to return against his will. And from both his letter to the Deputy Commissioner at Darjeeling, and the deed of assignment of the pony, it does not sound as though he asked or expected any more of them. All along, Maurice Wilson had understood and accepted the risk to his life. But whatever drove him, he had to go on; and if he could only do that alone, so be it. He did not know what was ahead; but, logical or not, he knew he could not go back.

Towards the end of August as the expedition team returned to Everest's lower slopes, below Camp III, and began reconnaissance work towards Karma Changri, Eric Shipton and Edwin Kempton sent their brief reports about finding Maurice Wilson's body to the British Political Officer, along with his diary and the few possessions they had kept back. The authorities in India were able to get the news to his mother back in England before the press ran the story the following month, confirming that the Englishman's body had been found. I imagine Sarah Wilson found it almost impossible to accept the finality of losing her son, after eighteen months of wondering, hoping, fearing and praying. Now all those conflicting emotions were replaced by grief for his lonely death on a far distant mountainside. She passed away herself the following year.

Following the work of the 1935 reconnaissance team, full climbing expeditions went to Tibet in 1936 and 1938 but were again unsuccessful, each experiencing appalling weather conditions. That was the end of a major chapter in Everest's history for, with dark clouds of war again looming over Europe, and the Tibetan government growing more fearful of foreign threats, there were no official expeditions to Everest for a further thirteen years.

After the Second World War, the Nepali authorities opened their country's borders. In contrast, China's invasion of Tibet in 1950 meant there was no longer any possibility of tackling the mountain from the north side.

Famously, Edmund Hillary and Tenzing Norgay reached the summit of Everest on 28 May 1953, and when the news broke their names flashed around the world. As Maurice Wilson had dreamed, they both became 'somebody', forever – with all the opportunities, and the pressures, that brings.

Fifty odd years on many still dream of climbing Everest. Most stay in their armchairs and rely on imagination, books and television. A few go part way, perhaps even as far as the climbers' monuments and prayer flags of one of the base camps. Fewer join climbing expeditions, and fewer still make it to the top. Even in these sophisticated times, they say around one in five trying for the summit will die.

In telling Maurice Wilson's story, for me the key climbs were by Reinhold Messner. With Peter Habeler, he initially reached the summit from Nepal on 8 May 1978, together the first men to get to the top without supplementary oxygen. But then, on 20 August 1980, having taken the same route up to the North Col as the British expeditions of the 1930s, Reinhold Messner became the first person to climb Everest alone. Again he did so without oxygen, and believed, like Maurice Wilson, that a small climbing team had just as good a chance as a large expedition. I find it both moving and fascinating that, as a very successful and experienced mountaineer himself, he was inspired, both before and during his second Everest climb, by the fitness, strength of will and determination of Maurice Wilson.

The Everest region of the Himalaya, on both sides of the mountain, has seen huge changes since the mystery and

romance of the attempts to reach the summit during the 1920s
and 1930s.

Once Nepal's borders had been opened a series of climbing expeditions sought permission to tackle many of the
world's greatest peaks. With imaginations tempted by tales
of Shangri-La, a few adventurous visitors followed behind
them, curious to see the formerly forbidden kingdom. Then
came the flower-power hippies, seeking their own enlightenment in the East, and tempted by everything Kathmandu
could offer. More recently trekkers have followed the routes
of mule trains and yaks up into the Himalayan foothills,
bringing employment, a cash economy and some material
wealth, but also great stress on a fragile landscape and a dramatic change to the traditional culture. In many places, satel-
lite dishes, Coca-cola and trainers reached villages years
before roads and wheeled transport. Despite all this, many
who visit Nepal are left with a profound impression not only
of the beauty of its scenery, but of the warmth, friendliness
and inner peace of many of its people.

Nepal's Khumbu region, which shelters below Everest,
long had close trading and religious links with Tibet. Dzatrul
Rinpoche was a renowned Buddhist teacher on both sides of
Chomolungma, and many of its people made a pilgrimage at
least once a year to gain his blessing, taking a tough but direct
path over the mountains to a point near the head of the
Rongbuk valley. Not only did he found Rongbuk, but he was
also the guiding influence in the establishment of
Thyangboche monastery, where many climbing Everest from
the Nepal side, including Edmund Hillary and Tenzing
Norgay back in 1953, seek the protection of the buddhas and
the gods before setting foot on the mountain. Khumbu is still
home to many Sherpa people and is a popular area for
trekking, and for some the employment it brings represents
the bountiful giving of Miyolangsangma. But in financial
terms, Nepal remains desperately poor, and since the sudden

death of King Birendra in 2001 has suffered from civil unrest and strife.

Following China's invasion of Tibet in 1950, the 'peaceful liberation' in May 1951 and the Dalai Lama's escape to Dharamsala in 1959, Tibet has changed completely. Estimates are that in the first twenty years of Chinese occupation 1.2 million Tibetans died in conflict, imprisonment, torture and through starvation as different farming techniques were imposed, often with disastrous consequences. Like their beloved Dalai Lama, many thousands fled over the mountains to India and Nepal, mostly on foot, hundreds not surviving the long, cold and desperately arduous journey. During the Cultural Revolution of 1966 to 1976, there was terrible suffering for most living under Beijing's rule. Tibetan culture and religion were brought to the brink of destruction; temples and monasteries were wrecked, monks and nuns imprisoned and tortured, and Buddhism denounced and outlawed.

Since the mid 1980s the Chinese authorities have gradually flooded Tibet with immigrants and I understand there are now 1.5 million more Chinese than Tibetans in the country with this figure growing all the time. In some areas, particularly Lhasa, Tibetans are vastly outnumbered. Refugees still risk the perilous trip over the mountains, with between 2,500 and 4,000 escaping each year. In September 2006, as I was writing this book, by chance a climbing team saw a group of these desperate people near the 19,000 ft (5,791m) pass of Nangpa La – which is on the old pilgrim route linking the Khumbu and Solu Khumbu villages with the holy Rongbuk valley – being shot at by Chinese soldiers. A young nun and a boy were killed, 32 of the little group were unaccounted for, and presumably taken by the army, but 41 made it across the border into Nepal, travelling from there to India.

The 2008 Beijing Olympics, and the Games' torch route over Everest, have once again focussed the world's attention on Tibet's occupation, and China's human rights and environmental record there. Although there are conflicting reports about what happened, and the fate of many involved will never be known, there is no doubting the strength of feeling of the Tibetan people, both there and in exile. And just a few weeks after the protests, the BBC reported on China's new education programme in Tibet to 'undermine support for the Dalai Lama and any separatist sentiment.'[16]

Although the March 2008 anniversary of the 1959 Tibetan uprising calls this into question, from outside the country it seems that power taken by guns and bullets is now mostly held through concrete buildings and China's consumer boom, with the new Beijing to Lhasa rail link being an ambitious tightening of the authorities' grip. And as Western nations and companies see China and its population as a massive developing market, so China has an eye on what foreign visitors can bring to its economy. Albeit on a much smaller scale than before 1950, some of Tibet's monasteries and temples have been restored to a degree and, although many precious books, paintings, statues and teachings are lost forever, some monks have been reinstated, restrictions on religious freedom have been relaxed within limits, and the tourists followed.

Dzatrul Rinpoche died in 1940. Trulshik Rinpoche succeeded him as the head lama of Rongbuk, but he and many of his monks had to flee to Nepal during the Cultural Revolution, seeking refuge and freedom to learn at the remote and beautiful hillside monastery of Thupten Choeling, in Solu Khumbu. Rongbuk itself was almost completely destroyed. When Reinhold Messner made his solo climb in 1980 he wrote that, other than the big chorten outside the main entrance, the place was in ruins. There has been some rebuilding since, and now a few monks live at Rongbuk, although Trulshik Rinpoche has not been able to return. As it did when Maurice Wilson was there, the monastery accommodates guests, although I suspect in a different atmosphere to that of the cheery warmth and sincere devotion he experienced.

For the governments of both Nepal and Tibet, fees from expeditions seeking to climb Everest are a useful source of revenue, although it seems most fees tend to go to central coffers rather than benefiting the local people. Following 1953, groups sought other routes to the summit, hungry for different climbing challenges. But more recently, with increased numbers of expeditions being allowed each year, often with relatively inexperienced climbers, and several teams following each other along the same route, the focus tends to be on getting as many up as possible, using tried and tested ways to the top. Sometimes this brings disastrous consequences, most famously in 1996 when fifteen people lost their lives. It has all put massive pressure on Everest's slopes, although commercial groups on both sides of the mountain are now in the main diligent about bringing their rubbish away, clean up teams have worked hard to deal with what was left before, and efforts have been made to cover bodies with stones.

While travelling in Tibet in 2005, I spent a chilly afternoon and night at Rongbuk.

As well as the low grey structure of the monastery guesthouse, with its peeling paint, infamous toilets and broken windows, there is a new Chinese hotel; and rickety wooden horse chariots and motorbikes carry tourists up to the first base camp, for there is a rough but driveable track all the way now. Ever the dreamer I had wanted to sense ghosts there; spirits of Wilson, and of Mallory and Irvine, Noel, Smythe, Warren and Shipton and of other names from the expeditions I had read about, who had passed that way. There had been heavy cloud all day, hiding Everest from both the Pang La, where we had stopped a few hours before, and the rocky

Rongbuk valley. Pitching our tents it felt scruffy, damp and a bit depressing – even having read Michael Palin's vivid description of his experiences there, the monastery was not as I had hoped.

Thinking of Dzatrul Rinpoche, and his blessing of Maurice Wilson, Tewang, Tsering, and so many others, I made my own pilgrimage to the monastery gompa. I found two rooms open; each had holy figures and geometric designs painted roughly on the walls, an altar and some simple statues. In one a stooped Tibetan lady, with a lined face, gold nose ring and traditional striped apron over her long black skirt, was taking down the offerings ready for evening, emptying water bowls into a bucket. She smiled warmly and nodded, stopping to watch me pad round clockwise in my walking socks.

There was a black and white photograph of a lama propped up on a wide low seat beside the offering table, khatas carefully draped round it. Trulshik Rinpoche most likely, I thought. Self consciously, I made my own offerings, paused for a few minutes and then headed back to our tents. Compared to older sacred places in Tibet, Rongbuk somehow lacks an ancient, dusty mystique, and the distinctive, heavy aroma and feel of the air that is left by incense and hundreds of butter lamps burning daily year after year. But its appeal comes from where it is, from the sacred valley and the great mountains, for what they have meant to so many for so long; and for all the feet that have tramped past it, and around it, whatever they came seeking.

That evening it got dark early, but after sunset some of the cloud lifted briefly. Miles away from the glow of streetlights, the sky was beautiful, full of stars, too many to count, and looking up the valley I strained my eyes, wanting there to be mountains in the faint moonlight. I was sure I could see a white triangular shape, and after a few minutes realised it was not moving like the clouds. I persuaded myself it was Everest, and did my best to hold the image in my memory in case that was all we saw. Shivering we headed for our sleeping bags, but slept fitfully, waking up cold and fighting for breath.

We got up before dawn. Struggling with numb fingers I dressed clumsily by torchlight, and then with my fleece zipped up and hat pulled over my ears I set off to base camp. Our little group straggled out, and for a while I walked on my own, plodding through the morning mist, trying to breathe steadily, with grey rocky moraine on either side of the track, a few prayer flags and the icy river, but other than patches of lichen almost no vegetation. Then the clouds began to move, parting little by little in front of an amphitheatre of mountains as sunshine lit a stage of snow slopes and brought out many subtle colours in rocks that, a few minutes before, had looked dull and lifeless.

It seemed only right that Everest should be the last to clear, and even then cloud hung stubbornly around the summit. At that point, glad to be alone, I tried hard to imagine Maurice Wilson also walking from Rongbuk, wondering how he had really felt. I was very conscious of being a tourist, with the benefit of films, travel programmes and guidebooks - and a return ticket to Heathrow.

At Rongbuk I had found it difficult to airbrush the modern trappings out of my mind's eye, but out there in the valley it was easier. Despite being passed on the track by horse chariots carrying visiting Chinese in green military greatcoats, who all waved and shouted, I had a sense of the sanctity of Chamlung, and of the mountain that dominates it. There was something about actually seeing it that all the pictures, books and television images could not have prepared me for. Whether you call it Chomolungma, Everest, Sagamartha or Qomolangma, if you are fortunate enough to see it, it is at once holy, majestic, awe inspiring and terrible. For me its immensity, with all its history and mysteries, was almost too difficult to take in.

There are two base camps now. Tourists are allowed to go as far as the first, where there is a noisy and colourful huddle of traditional Tibetan tents advertising food and basic accommodation, hawkers selling fossils and, bizarrely, a branch of China's post office. A few steps further on there is a climbers' monument, and many prayer flags tied together, some torn and faded, others bright and new. The second base camp is quite a distance on again, and is for climbing expeditions only.

It was strange, but as I stood in the sunshine looking towards the mountain, I could persuade myself that it did not look so far, and had a comfortably flat approach. In my mind's eye I pictured Maurice Wilson, thinking of his climbs up Lake District peaks, which can look steep and tough from below, and believing he could do it, feeling at once strong, confident and blessed. Now I understood just how deceptive the clear mountain air makes heights and distances. For some reason I remembered Peter Habeler's description of his last exhausting steps to the summit. 'I only thought in sensations and loose associations, and slowly I was overcome by the feeling that this threatening fearful mountain could be a friend. Today I am certain that it is in these positive and friendly sensations that the real danger on Everest lies.'[17] Perhaps these feelings seduced Maurice Wilson from afar, for even before he had reached Rongbuk, she had become another woman in his life. His last, and fatal, love.

WHAT'S PAST IS PROLOGUE

*The world is a better place because it contains
human beings who will give up ease and security in
order to do what they themselves think is worth
doing. They do the useless, the noble, divinely
foolish and very wisest things that are done by
man. And what they prove to themselves and to
others is that man is no creature of his habits, no
automaton of his routine, but that in the dust of
which he is made there is also fire, lighted now and
then by great winds from the sky.*

Walter Lipman

Maurice Wilson failed to climb Everest. But as an inexperienced airman and fell walker he flew alone over 5,000 miles
(8,047km), walked from northern India to Tibet and then
climbed up beyond 21,000ft (6,400m). To me, that was an
achievement. Others, with more technical training, equipment and practice, had previously got higher than this, and
obviously others since have got higher still, but at the time no
one had both reached the summit and come back. And
although by the end he must have thought his death was
inevitable, Maurice Wilson kept on trying.

Some have called him mad. Some have even said his lack
of equipment and experience meant his death was an elaborate suicide. Personally, I think that, like his flight to India,
Maurice Wilson meant to give climbing Everest his best shot,
to go for glory to show the world what he and his faith could
do. He was prepared to die trying if it came to it, and I sense

that even after his 'cure' he carried a desperation within him which perhaps meant he would risk more than most people; but I do not feel he went to Everest intending, or wanting, to die. If he had, why would he have returned to Rongbuk after his first attempt, or tried to persuade the Sherpas to help him climb higher during his second?

Certainly if Maurice Wilson had learned some practical climbing skills before leaving Europe, like cutting ice steps and using an axe, crampons and rope, as well as having the flying lessons he was required to take to qualify as a pilot, he would have given himself more of a fighting chance of getting up beyond the North Col. In his equipment, training and provisions he seriously underestimated what he was trying to achieve, and this is borne out by the completely unrealistic distances he thought he could climb in a day. However it seems to me that this lack of preparation came from naïve optimism rather than either reckless stupidity or a wish to die making a name for himself.

Maurice Wilson accepted that he had to learn to fly; but he already knew how to walk, and perhaps not realising what it would be like so high on Everest, and not appreciating what glaciers and snow slopes are like, he assumed that his ordinary walking skill, with sufficient physical fitness, would be enough. It was almost as though he felt he 'only' needed to be strong, determined and brave because his feet would be in familiar contact with the ground. And, to be fair, these qualities saw him through the long march from Darjeeling to Rongbuk and up past base camp. I imagine it must have been an almost unbearable shock to realise he was wrong. By that point he only had his faith to fall back on. There was nothing else. But probably there were times during his flight to India when he had felt something similar – and then he, or God, had pulled it off.

As Eric Shipton wrote, 'Either he had a perfect faith in the divine purpose of his mission or else preferred not to survive the bitterness of failure.' [1] Or perhaps there was both. In every age there are men and women who attempt amazing things of all kinds, testing human endurance, and trying to find out what we can achieve, develop or discover. Some fail, others succeed; some are denounced as crazy while a few are honoured as heroes. Given some of the desperate experiences of Maurice Wilson's life, the bleak unhappiness of his depression, and the pointless deaths he had seen in the trenches, I think he accepted all along that death could be the price for proving his theory – for making his dream reality. As his mother told journalists when he left England, 'My son is a very brave man.' [2]

Whether or not they think he was mad, and wherever they stand on the naïve versus reckless debate, most of those who have read a little of Everest's history at least join his mother in acknowledging Maurice Wilson's courage and determination. His story is almost stranger than fiction, and its fascination has persisted over the years, reappearing in different guises with similar regularity to the bundle of bones, which is all that is left of his body now, periodically exposed by the movement of the East Rongbuk glacier.

In the 1940s and 1950s, 'Wilson the Wonder Athlete' was a character in the *Wizard* comic. Spartan living and dedicated training made him unbeatable in a challenge. Perhaps the cartoon hero could trace his origin to another fruit and nuts man who shared the same surname. Certainly a story ran for several weeks, beginning on 8 October 1949, titled the *Forbidden Quest of the Man Named Wilson.* In that piece his goal was to reach the top of Everest, dodging the best efforts of the Dalai Lama's men to stop him. The serial ended with a passage describing a distant and mysterious look in Wilson's eye as he stumbled back to the tent he shared with his companion, dreamily explaining that he had promised the mountain he would keep it a secret if he reached the top.

A straight biographical account of Maurice Wilson's life, *I'll Climb Mount Everest Alone*, was published in 1957. It was written by journalist Dennis Roberts, who continued to advocate the Yorkshireman's achievements until his own death.

More recently, Barry Collins wrote a one-man play, *The Ice Chimney,* which was first presented in August 1980 and won the Edinburgh Festival's Fringe First Award. He looked for artistic inspiration beyond both the diary found with Wilson's body and Dennis Roberts' account, drawing on a theory that Maurice Wilson had a number of lovers, and played out a series of exotic sexual fantasies, sometimes also wearing women's clothing. The roots of this seem to have been in rumours that Eric Shipton and Dan Bryant hinted at finding a colourful second notebook describing these, along with items of women's underwear. The discovery of high heeled court shoe in fine brown leather, lying with a jumble of discarded oxygen gear and scattered tent poles, at one of the old English camps added fuel to the fire.

The play is powerful and moving. Through Barry Collins' words we hear a tormented, desperate Maurice Wilson speak in turn to the mountain, his embrace sometimes adoring but sometimes bitterly angry, the emotion almost overwhelming; to God, fighting doubts about his faith with each agonising and obsessive step; to 'his' women at home – 'Here's your nightdress, Sarah, your white nightdress – take it back love'; to his mother – 'I'm not coming home, mam... Try to understand' [3] – ; to his dead father and to Corbett, one of his companions from days facing death in the trenches. And at last, turning to look upwards again and summoning the strength for one last go, he calls to Chomolungma, hating her, loving her, but accepting that he will be forever tied to her, before his heart gives out.

It would have been good material for the tabloid headline writers, but I have not been able to trace any evidence that Maurice Wilson left a second notebook on Everest. Although the tale was attributed to Eric Shipton and Dan Bryant, there is no record of either man having written it down, and by the time it had become an urban myth they were both dead. Of course, anything said could well have been meant as a prank. The rumours might even have begun elsewhere – perhaps in Maurice Wilson's Wellington days for there may have been scandal or speculation around his divorce and hasty second marriage, or over him suddenly setting sail for England alone, possibly following a dispute with Ruby from who he was estranged, but not divorced, when he made his attempt on Everest. Certainly it seems that he had various girlfriends after his two marriages. New Zealander Dan Bryant may have heard something – he was known as a great source of anecdotes, and a playful hint, with a nod and a wink, can soon grow.

Alternatively the suggestion of another notebook may simply have come from the figure '3' written on the opening page of the one that is now in the Alpine Club's archives. I assumed that if there were volumes '1' and '2', they would have described the earlier stages of his journey, but someone else could have had a different thought.

Personally I do not believe Maurice Wilson had a second diary on Everest. Both Charles Warren and Edwin Kempson wrote clear and detailed records about finding Maurice Wilson's body and what was left of his tent and his rucksack; and neither of them mentioned either it or the underwear. Charles Warren said: 'Before disturbing the body we searched in the snow for his <u>notebooks</u> and other belongings'[4] (my underlining), but in describing what they found he uses the singular '...his diary ...', '...it ended...'

After Warren's initial discovery, the team worked together to hunt for Wilson's things and to bury their fellow climber.

It seems highly unlikely that any of them could have hidden something from the others – and it is hard to imagine why any of them would want to do so. In addition, all their accounts of reading the diary together that evening reflect there just being one document.

As for the lady's shoe, the reports came from the 1960 Chinese team which passed the various pre Second World War camps during their Everest attempt. However, apart from the weak link that he disguised himself in the long robes and sash of a local monk to travel through Sikkim and Tibet – not the traditional attire of the 1930s expeditions, but hard-ly womens' clothing – there is nothing to say that Maurice Wilson was a cross dresser, or to link the shoe to him, rather than to anyone else who had been high on Everest before 1960.

Mike Harding dismissed these rumours in his piece *Yorkshire Transvestite Found Dead on Everest.* 'The women's clothing, well even if it were true, everybody has to have a hobby. In any case is it not possible that Wilson, being a true northerner, was doing Everest the hardest way possible: in sling backs, liberty bodice and cami-knickers?'[5]

Again in fiction, Maurice Wilson made several guest appearances in Salman Rushdie's *The Satanic Verses*, first published in 1988. The novel is a kaleidoscope of colour, personalities, change and rivalry; presenting unexpected faces in the eternal war of good and evil. Drawing on the fable that the ghosts of those killed high on the mountains wander forever after death to guide living climbers the last stretch to the summit, Rushdie's character Alleluia Cone came across Maurice Wilson during her own Everest bid. He was sat on a glacier in the lotus position wearing immaculate black knickerbockers and a tartan tam-o'-shanter, and then casually strolled and floated beside her, chatting companion-ably and confiding his irritation over his remains having been stared at and filmed. Unbidden, other than perhaps by her own dream of climbing Everest alone, he follows Alleluia Cone back to London. There he appears periodically, high up amongst grey chimney pots and roof tiles – but still dressed in the tartan, which even in fiction, seems so unlikely for someone born into the Yorkshire wool trade.

Of course there have been theories around the extent of Maurice Wilson's Everest achievement, as well as the fictional accounts. From his diary we know that he reached a point just below the ice chimney up to the North Col (22 May 1934), and to within what he estimated to be about half a mile (0.8km) from the 1933 expedition's Camp IV, which was at around 22,710ft (6,922m), just below the crest of the North Col (25 May 1934), but nothing more definite than this.

Writing on the MountEverest.net website, American Thomas Noy, suggested that the world should look again at Maurice Wilson's climb, speculating that perhaps he did reach the summit. His rationale is based on an interview which he had in Lhasa with Gombu, a member of the 1960 Chinese expedition who told Noy that he had seen a pre Second World War tent at 27,887ft (8,500m), beyond what is known (from the rock colour) as the yellow band. He adds to this the fact that the crucial part of Wilson's shaving mirror was not found with the rucksack and other belongings near his body.

Noy wondered whether the tent could have been Wilson's, noting that if so, while he may not necessarily have reached the summit, he got far closer than had been previously thought. And might the absence of the mirror mean it had been left near that tent, or even higher still, perhaps having been used to signal to the monks at Rongbuk?

By coincidence, Thomas Noy met climber Mari Abrego in Lhasa in 1985. The leader of the Basque expedition was in the Tibetan capital sending home news of the death of his companion Juanjo Navarro on the North Col. As he was going back to Everest to bury his friend, Noy asked Mari

Abrego to look for Maurice Wilson's body in the area of the old Camp III. Mari Abrego found the Englishman's remains and took some photographs, which he duly sent to Thomas Noy. These included pictures of both what is left of his body and the slightly bent metal frame of a shaving mirror, but without the main reflective part of it.

Writer Jochen Hemmleb who, with Eric Simonson, interviewed Xu Jing the deputy leader of the 1960 Chinese expedition in 2001, argues that there are conflicts and approximations in the heights noted by members of the 1960 team, and wonders whether this accounts for the confusion. When that Chinese expedition reached the upper slopes of Everest, there were the remains of three pre Second World War camps there. The 1924 expedition's Camp VI at 26,706ft (8,140m) near the North ridge, the 1933 expedition's Camp VI at 27,473ft (8,380m) on the North East ridge and the 1938 expedition's Camp VI near the North East shoulder at 27,247ft (8,305m). From this interview and other research, Jochen Hemmleb believed that the mystery tent belonged to the 1938 expedition's camp VI, which was part way up the yellow band. He considered that although Maurice Wilson's strength and determination could have got him up onto the North Col, and even part way up the North ridge, he could not have made a serious bid for the summit.

It seems to me unlikely that any tent above Camp III would have been Maurice Wilson's. He, Rinzing and Tewang had two tents between them. The remains of one of those were found with his body, and I cannot imagine that once Rinzing and Tewang had made a decision to go down from Camp III they would have left a good tent behind, not when they had the long march back to Darjeeling ahead of them. It is true that at the time Tibetans and Nepalis frequently slept by the path in the open when they were travelling, or lodged in the villages or farms they passed, but especially over high passes and through uninhabited stretches, the chance of some shelter from the cold and biting wind would have been a valuable thing to the Sherpas.

As for the mirror, if Maurice Wilson had used it effectively high on the mountain, surely the monks at Rongbuk would have reported that. We know Dzatrul Rinpoche spoke of the Yorkshireman to members of the 1935 expedition. And Maurice Wilson's Union Jack was found in his rucksack near his body. If, by some miracle, he had reached the summit he would have left it there.

We will never know exactly how far up Everest Maurice Wilson climbed before he turned back to Camp III, and exhaustion, cold and exposure finally took their toll. Personally I doubt he had the climbing skill, or by that time the strength or energy, to get up to the top of the ice chimney and onto the North Col, and suspect that he did not live to see many, if any, days after his optimistic final diary entry.

While this may seem like a cop out, I – like Maurice Wilson, not a climber – do not feel it is so important to know precisely how far he got, for to me that is not the key part of his story. I agree he was naïve in not preparing adequately for his climb, and recognise that he did not take the 'sensible' alternative of going back when he could have done, but I respect his conviction in what he was doing, admire his strength and commitment, and applaud him for getting as far as he did. And, because the sensible way is not always, for everyone, the true way; having given all he could to make his crazy dream reality, to me at least he becomes a hero.

Despite the massive achievement of Edmund Hillary and Tenzing Norgay in 1953, and of all those who have reached the summit since them, some of the lasting public appeal and charm of Everest's climbing history still lies in the expeditions of the 1920s and 1930s, and the questions they left unanswered. Everyone has a view on the eternal conundrum of whether Mallory and Irvine really made it. His is another chapter in the tale, but Maurice Wilson is part of that history. He did not become known for reaching the summit, but he is famed for his audacious attempt, his colourful individuality and his determination to see it through. I think he would be quietly satisfied to know that. And I hope he could also find a wry smile both for his different fictional incarnations, and for the debate over how far he actually climbed. Perhaps, like Wilson the Wonder Athlete, he promised Chomolungma he would never tell.

After his own historic climb to the summit from Tibet in 1980, Reinhold Messner wrote, "The way is the goal' is a Buddhist saying, and mad as Wilson might seem, I have taken this persevering Don Quixote, who always carried with him in his rucksack some momentoes of the for him unattainable Enid Evans, to my heart. He is dearer to me than the legion of all those who anxiously build their little houses and pre-serve their lives for the old age pension.' [6]

To me, his words seem the best epitaph Maurice Wilson could have.

GLOSSARY OF TIBETAN WORDS USED

Bodhisattva – Someone motivated by great compassion who seeks enlightenment so that he or she may benefit all beings, and therefore dedicates his or her entire life, work and spiritual practice to this end. A superior bodhisattva (such as Chenrezig [Avalokiteshvara], the bodhisattva of compassion and Jampal Yang [Manjushri], the bodhisattva of wisdom), is an enlightened being who has completed all the stages of the path towards buddhahood and now strives to alleviate the suffering of others, and help them find liberation from the constant struggle of samsara.

Buddha – Essentially 'buddha' means 'awakened one', or 'the one who knows', someone who has seen through ignorance, is free from faults and understands how things really are. Many beings have become buddhas in the past and many more will become buddhas in the future. All beings have the capacity to become a buddha, but it may take many lifetimes for them to complete the path to enlightenment.

Chang – Rice wine/spirit.

Chenrezig – The bodhisattva of compassion (in Sanskrit, Avalokiteshvara) who is the most important deity in Tibet. He was born from a ray of white light from Buddha Amitabha, and given the task of working to alleviate the suffering of all beings. To do this he can take any shape and is aided by Green Tara and White Tara, who are themselves much venerated by Tibetan Buddhists. Chenrezig is often presented with eleven heads and a thousand arms, with an eye in the palm of each of his thousand hands. This is so that he can look out for suffering in every direction, contemplate different ways to help and then reach out many arms to do so. His mantra, Om mani padme hum, embodies the compassion and blessing of all the buddhas and bodhisattvas. Throughout countries in the Buddhist Himalayas it is painted, carved and printed on prayer flags, rocks, prayer wheels, walls and other places, and is chanted thousands of times daily. Reciting this mantra purifies and protects us from poisonous negative emotions and helps all beings reach true understanding.

Chorten – (In Nepal, stupa) – A square based structure with steps leading up to a dome and elaborate tiered finial or crown, which represents the buddhas' wisdom. They can be used to house holy relics. Miniature chortens, made of gold, silver and precious and semi precious stones, are often found inside temples and monastery buildings. Wherever they are, and whatever size, they are venerated, and walking clockwise around a chorten, while reciting mantras or other prayers, generates great merit.

Chupa – Long sleeved robe fastened at the waist with a belt, where it is pulled loose enough to make pockets for carrying things.

Dharma – Buddha's teachings, and the realisations that come from following them.

Dorje – (In Sanskrit, vajra) The diamond thunderbolt, used with a bell in Buddhist rituals to represent the spiritual path leading to the realisation of wisdom.

Dzong – In Tibet and in Bhutan, a building used in part as a fortress, in part as a centre of administration and in part as a place of worship or a monastery.

Dzongpen – Secular administrators in Tibet before the Chinese occupation.

Gompa – Temple, or a room, usually within a monastery or nunnery, where there is an altar, and holy rituals are carried out.

Gorak – Raven, believed by Tibetans to be messengers of the gods because they fly high up in the mountains.

Guru Rinpoche – (In Sanskrit, Padmasambhava). A great Buddhist master who was invited to Tibet from India in the eighth century by King Trisong Detsen to bring teachings and help to establish Tibet's first monastery at Samye. Before he could begin his task Guru Rinpoche subdued the spirits and forces of nature, which were central to the ancient Bon religion, and persuaded them to protect and support dharma teachings.

Khata – Fine white or cream scarf, sometimes worked with pictures of the eight auspicious Buddhist emblems. They are traditionally given as a greeting or farewell to those undertaking a journey, or as an offering to a holy image or teacher.

Kora – Circumambulating in a clockwise route around holy places while reciting mantras, and sometimes prostrating too. In Buddhist countries, going clockwise, or turning right, symbolises turning towards dharma.

Lama – A teacher of dharma. The various traditions of Tibetan Buddhism rely on spoken teachings, from lama to students, some of who later became teachers themselves, to preserve holy teachings, and the correct interpretation and understanding of them. The most senior teachers earn the title Rinpoche, and are revered with great devotion for the help and inspiration they give.

Lungta – Windhorse, carrying a precious stone surrounded by flames, which is believed to bring victory and grant wishes. They are traditionally shown on prayer flags and each movement of the flag sends the horse out into the wind, taking his precious load where it is needed.

Mantra – A Sanskrit word, literally meaning 'mind protection'. Mantras are repeated many times, either out loud or mentally, to protect the mind from delusions, and in praise and respect for holy beings.

Miyolangsangma – The Everest goddess, one of the Five Long Life Sisters who live on five Himalayan peaks. Originally a goddess of the Bon religion, she was converted to Buddhism by Guru Rinpoche. She is portrayed riding a tiger, holding in one hand a flower and in the other a bowl of food, symbolising inexhaustible giving.

Obos – Cairns or small towers built of loose stones, sometimes carved or painted with prayers. They are built on mountain passes as conciliatory offerings to the spirits that live there and a request for safe passage.

Puja – A ceremony of prayers and offerings; sometimes seeking blessings or help for a person or a certain undertaking, and sometimes for purification or in praise of a particular buddha or bodhisattva.

Samsara – The endless cycle of birth, death and rebirth through which sentient beings pass, deluded and distracted by false hopes and ambitions. Buddhas understood that ignorance is the basis of samsaric thought, and having gone beyond that, attained enlightenment. Trying to reach this awakening, and thereby liberation from samsara, is the goal of Buddhist practice. In the Mahayana tradition (the so called 'Great Vehicle', which is prevalent in Tibet and other countries in the Buddhist Himalayas) practitioners aim to gain enlightenment not only for themselves but for the benefit of all beings.

Buddha Shakyamuni – Buddha of the Present – Born Prince Siddhartha Gautama, he left his privileged life to seek spiritual truth, finally attaining enlightenment at what is now Bodhgaya in north-east India. For the next 45 years, until his death, he travelled with a small group of followers giving teachings so that others could also achieve enlightenment.

Torma – Intricately worked sculptures, in Tibet made of butter with lard and some flour, which are placed on altars as offerings, particularly when there are festivals or special ceremonies. Typically they are between 3in (11cm) and 12in (44cm) high, made in a conical or triangular shape leading up to a finial, decorated with butter rosettes and fluting. The butter is sometimes coloured with white, green, red and blue.

READING LIST

I am grateful to the authors and editors of the following books, whose words helped me to picture and understand some of Maurice Wilson's experiences, and to learn a little about flying, Tibet and climbing Everest.

ASTILL, T: *Mount Everest – The Reconnaissance 1935 – The Forgotten Adventure*, (2005) Published by the author
BONNINGTON, C: *Everest*, (2002) Weidenfield & Nicolson
CHICHESTER, F: *The Lonely Sea and the Sky,* (1967) Pan Books
CLARK, L: *The Marching Wind,* (1955), Hutchinson & Co.
DAVID-NEEL, A: *Tibetan Journey,* (First Indian Edition 1992) Book Faith India
ELIOT, T S: *Selected Poems* (1954) Faber
GILLMAN, P (Ed): *Everest – Eighty Years of Triumph and Tragedy*, (1993) Little, Brown & Company
GOODWIN, F: *The Flight of Wild Oats*, (1997) Carleton University Press
GYATSO, G K: *The Meditation Handbook*, (1995) Tharpa Publications
LEWIS, J (Ed): *The Mammoth Book of How It Happened – Everest*, (2003) Constable & Robinson
LUFF, D: *Amy Johnson – Enigma in the Sky*, (2002) Airlife Publishing
MESSNER, R: *The Crystal Horizon – Everest – The First Solo Ascent*, (1989) Crowood Press
MARKHAM, B: *West with the Night*, (1988) Penguin
NOEL, J: *Through Tibet to Everest*, (1927) Hodder & Stoughton

PEACOCK, J: *The Tibetan Way of Life, Death and Rebirth*, (2003) Duncan Baird

PALIN, M: *Himalaya*, (2004) Weidenfeld & Nicolson

ROBERTS, D: *I'll Climb Mount Everest Alone*, (1957) Robert Hale

RUTTLEDGE, H: *Everest – The Unfinished Adventure*, (1937) Hodder & Stoughton

RUSHDIE, S: *The Satanic Verses*, (1998) Vintage

SALKELD, A: *People in High Places*, (1991) Jonathan Cape

SALKELD, A and SMITH, R: *One Step in the Clouds*, (1990) Diadem

SCOTT, D: *Himalayan Climber*, (1992) Diadem

SHACKLETON, E: *The Polar Journeys* (2002) Collins Press

SMYTHE, F: *The Mountain Vision*, (1946) Hodder & Stoughton

SOGYAL RINPOCHE: *The Tibetan Book of Living and Dying*, (2002) Rider Books

TENZING NORGAY, J: *Touching My Father's Soul*, (2002) Random House

TENZING, J & T: *Tenzing and the Sherpas of Everest*, (2002) Robert Hale

VENABLES, S (Ed): *Everest – Summit of Achievement – Royal Geographical Society*, (2003) The Book People – Ted Smart

WILLIS, M: *Tibet – Life, Myth and Art*, (1999) Duncan Baird

Other source material included information from the following websites - The Tibet Society, MountEverest.net, The Science Museum, BBC News and The Long Long Trail; as well as Maurice Wilson's diary and extracts from the diaries of Edwin Kempson, Charles Warren and Edmund Wigram from the Alpine Club's archives; newspaper cuttings and the India Office file on Maurice Wilson held in the British Library.

REFERENCES

References are to quotations taken from items other than Maurice Wilson's diary

They called him the Mad Yorkshireman
1. Third supplement to the *London Gazette* of Friday, 13 September 1918 (date of entry – Monday, 16 September 1918)

Mountains, myths and mystery
1. *Everest: Summit of Achievement* edited by Stephen Venables – page 11
2. *Everest: Summit of Achievement* edited by Stephen Venables – page 126

Ambition airborne
1. *The Lonely Sea and the Sky* by Francis Chichester – page 66
2. *Daily Sketch*, 25 April 1933
3. Letter from Mr L V Heathcote, Burmah-Shell Oil Storage and Distributing Company, Calcutta to Mr Tymms, Director of Civil Aviation in India dated 2 May 1933 (British Library)
4. Letter from Maurice Wilson to the Deputy Director of Civil Aviation, London dated 10 May 1933 (British Library)
5. Telegram from Air Ministry to Maurice Wilson sent 16 May 1933 (British Library)
6. *Sunday Pictorial*, 23 April 1933
7. *The Mammoth Book of How it Happened – Everest* edited by Jon E Lewis - page 437 (and *The People*, 22 July 1934)
8. *The Mammoth Book of How it Happened – Everest* edited by Jon E Lewis - page 437 (and *The People*, 22 July 1934)
9. *The Mammoth Book of How it Happened – Everest* edited

by Jon E Lewis - page 438 (and *The People*, 22 July 1934)
10. Report of Lieut Col Gordon Loch, Political Agent, Bahrain dated 6 June 1933 (British Library)
11. Political Department Minute on private fliers and the Arab Air Route dated 17 August 1933 (British Library)

Marking Time

1. *The Mammoth Book of How it Happened – Everest* edited by Jon E Lewis - page 438 (and *The People*, 22 July 1934)
2. *Daily Express*, 9 June 1933
3. Telegram from Foreign Office, Simla to British Envoy, Nepal dated 3 June 1933 (British Library)
4. *The Mammoth Book of How it Happened – Everest* edited by Jon E Lewis - page 438 (and *The People*, 22 July 1934)
5. *The Standard*, 10 June 1933
6. *The Mammoth Book of How it Happened – Everest* edited by Jon E Lewis - page 439 (and *The People*, 22 July 1934)
7. *The Mammoth Book of How it Happened – Everest* edited by Jon E Lewis - page 440 (and *The People*, 22 July 1934)
8. *I'll Climb Mount Everest Alone* by Dennis Roberts – page 84
9. Report of Mr A D McDonald Clark, Deputy Commissioner, Darjeeling, 2 May 1934 (British Library)
10. Statement of Tewang Bhutia (undated but made following the Sherpas' return to Darjeeling on 7 July 1934) (British Library)

Into Tibet

1. *The Crystal Horizon* by Reinhold Messner – page 126
2. *The Mammoth Book of How it Happened – Everest* edited by Jon E Lewis - page 128

The First Attempt

1. *Everest: Eighty Years of Triumph and Tragedy* edited by Peter Gillman - page 22
2. *Mount Everest – The Reconnaissance 1935 – The Forgotten Adventure* by Tony Astill - page 173
3. *Everest: Eighty Years of Triumph and Tragedy* edited by

Peter Gillman - page 25

4. *Through Tibet to Everest* by John Noel - page 169
5. *Through Tibet to Everest* by John Noel - pages 160-161
6. *The Crystal Horizon* by Reinhold Messner – pages 149-150

A Break at Rongbuk

1. *Everest: The Unfinished Adventure* by Hugh Ruttledge - page 286
2. *Through Tibet to Everest* by John Noel - page 141
3. *Through Tibet to Everest* by John Noel - pages 198-199

A Second Go

1. *Through Tibet to Everest* by John Noel - page 178
2. *Through Tibet to Everest* by John Noel - pages 178-179

The Last Effort

1. *The Crystal Horizon* by Reinhold Messner – pages 227-228
2. *South: The Story of Shackleton's Last Expedition 1914-1917* (from The Polar Journeys) page 156
3. *The Waste Land* by T S Eliot: What The Thunder Said – line 362
4. *Everest: Eighty Years of Triumph and Tragedy* edited by Peter Gillman page 156

The Final Chapter

1. Statement of Tewang Bhutia (undated but made following the Sherpas' return to Darjeeling on 7 July 1934) (British Library)
2. Letter from Maurice Wilson to the Deputy Commissioner at Darjeeling dated 17 May 1934, written at Camp III and given to Tewang (British Library)
3. Statement of Tewang Bhutia (undated but made following the Sherpas' return to Darjeeling on 7 July 1934) (British Library)
4. *Daily Mail*, 20 July 1934
5. *Daily Mail*, 21 July 1934
6. Letter from Mr A McDonald Clark, Deputy

Commissioner, Darjeeling to Mr F Williamson, Political Officer, Sikkim dated 2 August 1934 (British Library)
7. *Mount Everest – The Reconnaissance 1935 – The Forgotten Adventure* by Tony Astill – page 4
8. Charles Warren's diary (Alpine Club archives)
9. Charles Warren's diary (Alpine Club archives)
10. Charles Warren's diary (Alpine Club archives)
11. Edwin Kempson's diary (Alpine Club archives)
12. Edmund Wigram's diary (Alpine Club archives)
13. *Mount Everest – The Reconnaissance 1935 – The Forgotten Adventure* by Tony Astill – page 172
14. *Everest: The Unfinished Adventure* by Hugh Ruttledge pages 20-21
15. *Mount Everest – The Reconnaissance 1935 – The Forgotten Adventure* by Tony Astill – page 174
16. http://news.bbc.co.uk/1/hi/world/asia-pacific - 21 April '08
17. *Everest: Eighty Years of Triumph and Tragedy* edited by Peter Gillman - page 109

What's Past Is Prologue
1. *Mount Everest – The Reconnaissance 1935 – The Forgotten Adventure* by Tony Astill – page 173
2. *I'll Climb Mount Everest Alone* by Dennis Roberts – page 59
3. *The Ice Chimney* by Barry Collins – reproduced in *One Step in The Clouds* compiled by Audrey Salkeld and Rosie Smith – pages 351 and 361
4. Charles Warren's diary (Alpine Club archives)
5. *Yorkshire Transvestite Found Dead on Everest* by Mike Harding - pages 14-17
6. *The Crystal Horizon* by Reinhold Messner – page79

ILLUSTRATIONS

If not stated otherwise, photographs were taken by George Rhodes or Ruth Hanson

ABOUT THE AUTHOR

Like Maurice Wilson, Ruth Hanson was born and brought up in Bradford. Since 1991, she has travelled fairly widely in the Himalayas, mainly in Nepal but also visiting Tibet, Sikkim and Bhutan. She currently works as an in house lawyer, and lives with her partner in North Yorkshire.

COMMUNITY ACTION NEPAL

In 1975, Doug Scott and the late Dougal Haston became the first British climbers to reach the top of Mount Everest. Doug later co-founded the registered charity Community Action Nepal, wanting to help the people from a country that is so 'emotionally wealthy' that it makes an impact on almost everyone who goes there, but has little of what we generally think of as 'wealth' in the Western world – few educational opportunities and scant access to primary health care or clean water systems.

CAN funds projects, the majority of which are in the middle hill region of Nepal. This area sees little benefit from the tourist industry and the people there are amongst the poorest in Nepal. The projects, mainly schools, health posts, clean water supplies, community development and vocational training programmes are established following negotiations with village committees. Villagers are asked to contribute approximately one third of a project's costs, usually by way of labour and building work supervised and guided by CAN staff. On completion the project is handed over to the committee and is run as an integral part of village life, although there is ongoing support from CAN when and where necessary. CAN continues to select, train and pay salaries to the teachers and nurses involved, to advise where appropriate on community development and to train villagers to be increasingly self-sufficient.

I have seen the work of two of CAN's key projects during visits to Nepal. The first was in 1999 when I visited the already well established school at Ghunsa, which is in the Solu Khumbu area. Our trekking group had a warm and humbling welcome – if any of us had not appreciated it before, we soon realised what a big difference CAN had already made to families in the area. Having seen the serious side of this work, with classrooms fully occupied and lessons under way, we spent a noisy and memorable evening in the open playground as people came out of the darkness from homes and farms up and down the hillside to share music, laughter and dancing.

The second was in 2001, in the Sankhuwasawa district to the south of Khumbakarna Himal. The small and remote settlement of Walung stretches along one steep side of the narrow Arun river valley with views north towards the mountains. While I was there CAN was supporting work to reconstruct the village gompa (monastery), and building was already well under way. We camped on field terraces above piles of wood and boulders, waking each morning to the sound of stone masons' chisels, and the smell of incense as the local lama sat under a colourful archway of prayer flags chanting prayers for the success of the work. The gompa is finished now. A temporary health post was established in it in 2004 and it is planned that by the end of 2007 this will move to a purpose built and permanent home.

Community Action Nepal (registered charity number 1067772) can be contacted in the UK at Warwick Mill, Warwick Bridge, Carlisle, CA4 8RR. More information on CAN and its work is available from www.canepal.org.uk.